# Restaurants and Tales / Reha Tanör

Editor: Stefan Martens
Content Manager: Esin Aksoy Yılmaz
Design by: Erhan Güven & Brand The Bliss
Art Director: Serdar Akyıldız
Graphic Design: Tuğba Gülgüler
Creative Technologist: Emre Koç
Publishing Coordinator: Esra Mutlu
Digital Communication Adviser: Ercüment Büyükşener

Culinary Adviser: Nurdan Tanör

*With special thanks to Nejat Çifçi*

# RESTAURANTS
## *and*
# TALES

# Index

I'M GOING TO BE A PIMP WHEN I GROW UP (Omotesando Hill, Tokyo)...... 6

WHAT TRANSPIRED AFTER THE OFFICE PARTY (Dowtown Cipriani, New York)...... 10

DESSERT FIRST AT ALAIN DUCASSE (Alain Ducasse At Plaza Athenée, Paris)...... 12

MISERY: THE ARTIST'S INSPIRATION (Klimataria, Athens)...... 14

THE MAN WHO SLIPPED INTO MY WIFE'S ROOM (Oak Room, New York)...... 16

THE BENTLEY AT THE DOOR OF THE POGGIO (Poggio, Sausalito (California))...... 18

MISSING THE SUNSET AT DA GELSOMINA (Da Gelsomina, Capri)...... 24

THE WOMEN'S HAMAM (Solbar, Napa Valley)...... 26

THE BENEFITS OF WALKING (La Pergola, Rome)...... 28

IF YOU'RE GOING TO DO A JOB, DO IT RIGHT (Chez Janou, Paris)...... 30

ON WHAT MARRIED WOMEN SUFFER FROM THE LANGUAGE OF MEN (Carlton Beach, Cannes)...... 32

THE OCEAN OF ANISA AND ASLAN (Grill Garden, Bodrum)...... 34

ARE ALL THE GINAS IN ITALY BEAUTIFUL? (Osteria Le Logge, Siena)...... 36

YOU'RE THE WOMAN OF MY BED! (Bebek Balikçi, Istanbul)...... 38

THE PARADISE OF IL RICCIO AFTER THE INFERNO OF THE MARINA GRANDE (Il Riccio, Capri)...... 40

DINNER BY HESTON BLUMENTHAL AND LA BOHÈME (Dinner By Heston Blumenthal, London)...... 44

I WASN'T CUT OUT TO BE A VIOLINIST (Na Cosu, Belgrade)...... 48

A TASTING MENU IS LIKE A FASHION SHOW (Zelmira, Modena)...... 52

THE MUSICIAN WITHOUT LISTENERS (Locanda Di Sant'Agostino, San Gimignano)...... 54

THE TOWN WITH STREETS THE SCENT OF CITRUS (Kortan, Bodrum)...... 56

WHAT'S "NORMALE" IN PORTOFINO AND "NORMAL" IN ADANA (The Stella, Portofino)...... 58

ON EASILY CONVINCED HUSBANDS AND CUSTOMERS (Dva Jelena, Belgrade)...... 62

CONCHIGLIA THE DESTINATION, IL POSTINO THE CONSOLATION (Il Postino, Procida Island)...... 66

THE ATELIER ROBUCHON AND THE MICHELIN CRITERIA (Atelier Robuchon, Paris)...... 70

WHAT KIND OF MAN WOULD YOU LIKE? (Le Balcon, Paris)...... 74

LUNA CAPRESE AT LE GROTELLE (Le Grotelle, Capri)........................................................ 76

A LITTLE PAIR OF SOCKS (Cafe Arlequin, San Francisco)................................................. 78

HARRY'S BAR STILL CAPITALIZING ON LA DOLCE VITA (Harry's Bar, Rome)................. 80

THE SHARES IN THE ELEVATOR (Stone Tavern, New York)............................................... 82

EGGPLANT GROWERS AREN'T PAYING MY SALARY! (Fiorello, New York)....................... 84

WOMAN CHEFS' "SOFT SPOT" FOR CHILDREN (La Dame De Pic, Paris)......................... 86

HOW DID I DIRECT TRAFFIC AT THE WASHROOMS AT GEORGES? (Georges, Paris)...... 88

THE ELEGANCE OF THE MAÎTRE D' AT BLUE HILL (Blue Hill At Stone Barns, New York).......... 92

A PASTRY FOR SOME, A PASTING FOR OTHERS FROM RITA HAYWORTH (Le Pavillon Eden Roc, Cap D'antibes).94

IN PURSUIT OF STOLEN PRIDE (Bernardin, New York)..................................................... 96

WHY DID MARILYN MONROE KISS MY FATHER? (Gaonnuri, New York)......................... 100

MY ADVENTURE WITH CAVIAR RISOTTO AT OSTERIA FRANCESCANA (Osteria Francescana, Modena).104

THE LITTLE BLOND BOY (Ristorante Nino, Rome)........................................................... 108

THE RESTAURANT OF THE NIGHT OF HORROR (Max, Auburn (California))..................... 112

HAVE YOU EVERY MISSED THE BALLET FOR A MEAL? (Relais Plaza, Paris)................... 114

VON KARAJAN AND PER SE (Per Se, New York)............................................................. 118

RUNNING INTO SYLVIE VARTAN AT LE STRESA (Le Stresa, Paris).................................. 122

MEMORIES OF CANNES ESCAPADES AT LE DIVELLEC (Le Divellec, Paris).................... 124

RUNNING THE RULE ON MY FAVORITE RESTAURANTS (New York, London, Paris, San Francisco).........126

THE BRIDE FROM ROME (Al Moro, Rome)..................................................................... 130

FROM LE RELAIS TO İSMET BABA (Le Relais, Lugano)................................................... 134

MY RESTAURANT EVALUATION MANIFESTO AND LE CLARENCE (Le Clarence, Paris)............138

THE CARPENTER AND THE AMERICAN (Orfoz, Bodrum)................................................ 140

DO SILK SHIRTS EAT SOUP? (Peter Lugar, New York).................................................... 142

IS THIS PLACE GOING TO FLOOD? (Wolseley, London).................................................. 144

THE 8-YEAR-OLD FUGITIVE (Beyti, Istanbul) ................................................................ 146

# I'm Going To Be A Pimp When I Grow Up

## Omotesando Hill, Tokyo

My mother and father split up when I was still very young – I don't even remember it. Until I went to boarding school, I spent some of my time with my mother and some of it with my father.

My mother was an authoritarian woman, while my father, despite being in the military, was a far softer touch. Whenever I went to spend time with him, I'd have a lot of fun, staying with his officer friends. Just 4 or 5, I was a small, blond kid who liked playing and wrestling "with the boys."

Usually, you would ask a small child his or her name when you first met them. The second question was always about which school they were going to and which grade they were in. If, perchance, they were not yet in school, the stand-in question was this:

"What are you going to be when you grow up?"

Whenever I was with my mother, I would say that I was going to be the captain of the Yavuz, the most magnificent battleship in the navy's fleet. As far as I know, it had been involved in some heroic activity in World War I that was retold like a legend.

Whenever I went to my father's place, his officer mates would teach me things that I hadn't seen at my mother's place, one of which was my future "occupation." On this front, they rigorously enjoined me regarding one occupation, making me repeat it time and time again to see if I was pronouncing it correctly.

"When people ask, say that you are going to be a pimp when you grow up!"

"OK."

"If anyone asks why, make sure you say 'it's a very respectable occupation, that's why.' Right then, let's hear you say it one more time!"

I repeated the phrase. They broke into fits of laughter and took a sip of their rakı. One time, they even gave me a bit, saying it was water. Everything was different with men who were preparing to go to war and die. I liked this difference and had a lot of fun with them.

My father was the commander of an artillery brigade that was set to participate in the Korean War. One day, we were coming back from some military exercises and had stopped for a break by the side of the road. As we were drinking from a fountain, a car stopped beside us.

"Wow, the chief," they said.

It was the mayor. The mayor exited the vehicle, along with his three daughters, who were quite young and beautiful. Seeing a blond, rotund child amid the herd of officers, they made a beeline toward me and started to pinch and kiss me. After the physical harassment had been completed, the questions began:

"What's your name?"

I responded.

As they were going through the list, the question that was a fixture in the repertoire arrived:

"So, tell us, what are you going to be when you grow up?"

With my chest filling with pride, I said what I had learned from the officers:

"I'm going to be a pimp!"

"What?!?! What kind of thing is that to say?" they exclaimed in shock, bringing their hands to their open mouths.

I felt the need to elaborate further:

"Because it's a very respectable profession!"

I don't remember the rest. As it is, close to 70 years have passed.

The incident came to mind again years later as I was having a bite at a café-restaurant in Tokyo. A cute robot had welcomed us. It asked us our name and then said "welcome."

But it got me thinking: robots are programmed; what if the things that it learns are like the things that I learned when I was young? Can you imagine what would happen?

"So tell me, what's your name?"

"Robot X."

"What are you going to be when you grow up, Robot X?"

"I'm going to be a pimp!"

"What?!?! Whatever for?"

"It's a very respectable profession, that's why!"

I started to laugh, but my wife immediately stepped in to control the situation: "Don't laugh all on your own; they'll think you're crazy!"

I took a sip of my sake and related the story. She started to laugh too...

I don't remember the name of the café-restaurant – it was an enjoyable place in the Omotesando Hills complex, with lots of books on the walls.

I broke into a fit of laughter again on the way out.

"Why are you laughing again this time?" my wife asked.

"As soon as we get to San Francisco, I'm going to teach Aslan (my 3-year-old grandson) about what he's going to be when he grows up!"

"Don't you dare!" my wife admonished me. As if that wasn't enough, she waved her finger at me and repeated her stern warning.

"When I was a child," I said, "The most desirable occupations were to be an officer or a civil servant. When I was in my youth, being a doctor, an engineer and a lawyer came to the fore. I wonder what young mothers and fathers want their children to become now?"

> 66 "So, tell us, what are you going
> to be when you grow up"?
> With my chest filling with pride,
> I sad what I had learned from the
> officers: "I'm going to be a pimp". 99

# What Transpired After The Office Party ?

## Dowtown Cipriani, New York

Our office party this year was quite a different affair. In the past, we always used to get in catering, but this year, my assistant decided on something new, instructing everyone to bring something "they made themselves." The only things people were allowed to buy were booze and a bit of snack food.

The upshot? It was wonderful. Who knew our employees and guests were so talented? Every one of them rustled up something unique to eat or drink – to the extent you could have never found such variety on a catering menu.

We enjoyed the proceedings, but I got up to go home at 8, leaving our younger contingent to get on with the fun. As I was leaving, my assistant pressed a bag into my hand.

"Here's a little something for your wife," she said. "I do wish she could have come..."

"What'd you put in the bag?" I asked.

"I made a note of what you liked the most tonight and prepared a selection."

My wife was overjoyed at the leftovers on offer. And naturally, there is a tradition for us – and perhaps with yourselves as well: If someone prepares something by hand for you, you never return their plate empty. Instead, you make something as well, put it on the plate and send it back...

So that's exactly what my wife did. A couple of days later, she put a wonderful cake on the plate my assistant had used and prepared to send it on its way.

"I put the plate in a bag. I'll put it by the door tonight – don't forget it in the morning!"

When I got up the day after, my wife was still sleeping. As I was leaving, there were two bags by the door; I took the larger one and headed off to work.

When I got to the office, I gave the bag to my assistant. "My wife thanks you a lot! She made this... 'I hope she likes it!' she said."

Not long after, my assistant poked her head in my door. She was making a valiant attempt to appear furious, but it was clear to all concerned that she was trying hard not to laugh.

"What was it that your wife said?" she inquired.

"'I hope she likes it!'" I replied.

She delved further: "The things she sent?"

"Yes, of course," I answered. "She prepared it especially for you!"

Unable to maintain the charade any longer, my assistant soon gave herself up.

"Sir, the bag you brought is full of garbage!" she revealed.

"What garbage are you talking about?" I retorted.

"I swear to God... Take a look for yourself!"

As I gawked at the bag, my phone rang – it was my wife.

"I hope you didn't give her the bag!" my wife said as soon as I answered the phone.

"I did..."

"Well, you just went and took the garbage I had left by the door!" she admonished me. "The bag with the cake is still sitting here. Really, I don't know what I'm going to do with you. This is so humiliating."

To be truthful, I didn't know what I was going to do with myself. As it was, I had joined the ranks of the septuagenarians with this office party and I sometimes wondered if my mind was starting to go. My tastes, too, were changing, and I was increasingly finding myself a fan of more casual parties and casual restaurants. At places like that, there's no need for a jacket and tie – everyone is more at ease.

The Cipriani Downtown in New York is one such restaurant. A Cipriani was opened in Istanbul, but the serious ambiance there was a far cry from the casualness in New York. In Istanbul, Cipriani's snooty waiters acted as if they were waiting tables at Jean Georges. Of course, it didn't fly, and the Cipriani in Istanbul soon closed down.

Of the several Ciprianis in New York, my favorite is the one in Soho. The food isn't really anything to write home about – but when the menu is this broad, one can hardly expect fantastic fare.

Still, there's no reason to complain. What I liked most was the baked tagliolini with ham, which is also a specialty of Harry's Bar. The Eggplant alla Parmigiano, however, was not as good as it is in Rome – perhaps because of the different eggplant.

However, I can recommend the Mediterranean Branzino al forno. And anyone going there must down a traditional Bellini cocktail.

The restaurant might be a bit noisy, but it's a place you'll feel comfortable in. Actually, if I'm going to admit it, the best thing about it might be the chance to engage in some people watching – especially, if I may say so, the many beautiful women in attendance. You really wonder whether all the Big Apple's youngest and prettiest frequent the bars and restaurants of Soho or, more to the point, whether there's a rule that they have to do so...

# Dessert First At Alain Ducasse

## Alain Ducasse At Plaza Athenée, Paris

If you're curious about expensive restaurants and want to stay at luxury hotels but your budget isn't going to let you play along, then you should devise tactics like mine to find the path of cheapest resistance!
I learned that every poison had an antidote from Madame Gavard, the chemistry teacher who failed me. I don't remember now but maybe it was my physics teacher, Monsieur Butery – who also failed me – who actually said it…
Since I can't remember if the saying is associated with chemistry or physics, it comes as no surprise that I constantly flunked in school.
Since some restaurants are very expensive and you are presented with the most contemptuous of glances from waiters when you order the cheapest dishes or cheapest wine, there are always ways to fight back.

Every poison has an antidote!

I have a few tactics, so I'll let you in on a couple of secrets. If you know of similar methods, please share them with me so that we can establish "a fraternity of eating cheap at expensive restaurants without being insulted."

My first method is to take advantage of religious taboos.
Before I arrive at a restaurant, I do a bit of pre-drinking wherever I am. While the waiter fills your glass with water and asks if you'd like an aperitif after placing the wine list on the table, I immediately object:
"No alcohol… No pork…"
The man instantly removes the wine list, all while cursing his luck to have been dealt one of those problem customers, but he'll keep quiet in order to avoid making more trouble for himself.

Alcohol is usually the most expensive item on the bill. What's more, it's evil... It's bad for your health... So by avoiding a drink, you're killing two birds with one stone.

The second method is based on diet. God bless those dieticians and people who work in this field. We have been subjected to such a dietary bombardment in the media, with them constantly telling us, "Eat this, don't eat that – oh wait – eat THIS, not THAT," that when you tell your waiter that you're on a diet, he probably won't have the strength to challenge you. Because most probably he's on a diet too... If not him, then his wife or daughter are certainly consuming probiotic yoghurt for dinner.

You have to admit that the first method I hatched to order little without being insulted by the waiter is highly original.
The second one might be recognized by the public and be very popular – something that I accept.

But the third one is all mine, a sui generis method. I don't think you've even thought about it.

I sit at the table... The waiter arrives... Looking at me, he already guesses that I won't be ordering anything expensive, but at this point he maintains his composure. He pours my mineral water. He asks if I would like an aperitif, I say no... As he tries to shove the wine list in my face, I ask:
"What's for dessert?"
Nothing can stop the waiter from being baffled at this question. As he tries to make sense of it all, he says:
"Does Monsieur want to know about our desserts?"
I look straight at him:
"Yes, please... As it happens, I'm crazy about desserts and I'd like to see what's on the menu. If perchance you have something I like, I can only order one main dish. If your dessert menu isn't all that good, I could go for an entrée, main course and just one small dessert."

The waiter is stupefied. In all his life as a waiter, he probably hasn't come across someone ordering backwards. That's why he politely serves you, fetches the dessert menu or recites it for you!
As you may have guessed, the desserts of the restaurant are very important to me. I order the cheapest dessert and a main course and finalize the deal victoriously.

I also used this method at Alain Ducasse. There was just one thing I didn't take into account: The wit of the waiter:
"Since Monsieur has ordered dessert first, would he like me to start with that?"

Yes, every poison has an antidote, but you have to admit that it's not easy to match wits with the waiters of Paris!

# Misery: The Artist's Inspiration

## Klimataria, Athens

I really wanted to be an artist, but it wasn't to be.

When I was in high school, I was selected to play the lead role in a theatrical play. But shortly after the rehearsals began, the director came and told me he wanted to give me a "more important" character role; devoid of any other option, I accepted.

Not long thereafter, the director came back and said: "You're wasting your talents in being an actor. If you become the director's assistant, it'll really add something to the piece." Again devoid of any other option, I accepted, "adding something" to the piece by printing the invitations and painting the décor...

I thought I'd try my hand at poetry. I wrote one poem that took some inspiration from a Shakespearean sonnet — and even borrowed a few pompous words from the English bard — before proceeding to read it to the girl whom I had my eagle eye on. All she said when she listened to me was "you're really funny." I got the message.

I gave myself over to novels, choosing to pen something about a refugee's adventurous journey. I had my asylum-seeking youth surreptitiously board a freighter bound for New York and began to tell the story. After a while, I had a look and realized that I had passed page 50 and the boat hadn't even weighed anchor! At this rate, my book was going to give the Russian classics a run for their money. That, however, would be a disservice to them — if truth be told, I had even started to get bored, so I left it there. I had my youth disembark the boat and sent him back to his family (for some reason, it had never occurred to me to send my protagonist off to New York together with his family).

Writers typically graduate from the short story to the novel; I, however, did the exact opposite. My first short story was titled The Hair in My Shaver Is Truly Unhappy. If you ask me, it was an experiment worthy of Sartre, but my literature teacher wasn't quite of the same opinion. "My son, why don't you try shaving with a razor?" he asked; after that, I gave that up too. But by then, school had finished, so there was no time left to write.

Apparently, then, there might have been two reasons why I failed to become an artist:
1) I didn't have the talent.
2) I hadn't experienced enough misery!

After all, an artist's inspiration is misery. Isn't it melancholy, pain and misery that have driven the vast majority of artists – the novelists we read, the composers we listen to and the painters we follow – to create their works? Ultimately, I determined that I hadn't succeeded in becoming an artist because, thanks be to God, I didn't have those kinds of problems.

One of the branches of art in which misery is most prevalent is undoubtedly music. And in music, few genres are so marked by misery as rebetiko. In the 1920s, the Greeks of Anatolia and the Turks of Greece were subjected to a mutual population exchange. People were uprooted from their homes, places of work and soil before being packed off to an unknown world. Naturally, they expressed their pain in song, and close to 100 years later, they're still singing these songs, because pain doesn't fade easily...

Rebetiko music is frequently played in the meyhanes of Athens and Istanbul, although the style of music in many of these tavernas has been watered down, becoming a bit touristy. That's why it's not easy to find authentic rebetiko. Athens' Klimataria Tavern is one of the rare meyhanes where you can still find rebetiko in its rawest and purest form. There are just three drinks on the menu: wine, rakı and ouzo.
The portions of food, meanwhile, are big, but if you're going to ask about them, let me just tell you this: You didn't come here to eat, you came here to hear real rebetiko.
The music starts toward 11 with a five-person group, all of whom both play and sing. The woman in the middle happens to have the most moving voice. While performing, they occasionally take sips from small glasses of straight rakı to wet their palate and wet their lips. Is it possible to have rakı straight? Not really, but it's probably not really possible to hit the stage and dig into meze at the same time. That's why they make do with just a cigarette – one of them even rolled their own as the music continued. The smoking continues, as they light one where the other finishes. Whenever they take a drag on a cigarette while singing, they miss the note – but there's nothing to worry about. Their music is of spectacular melancholy and beauty. They take everyone in the house back and forth to other worlds.

After starters of mashed broad beans, as well as crushed and fried eggplant, you can continue with some of His Majesty's Favorite (Hünkar Beğendi) and eggplant with minced meat (karnıyarık) featuring cumin and béchamel sauce – not because any of it is really good, but because you're not going to make it through the whole night just drinking alcohol!

But music is food for the soul, so feed yourself with the strains of rebetiko for an evening. You certainly won't regret it...

# The Man Who Slipped Into My Wife's Room

## Oak Room, New York

It was way back in the 70s…

There were no cell phones, internet, email, Google or Tripadvisor in those days. Needless to say, it was never a walk in the park to make a hotel reservation in a foreign country…

I had gone to Atlanta for a fair before heading to New York for a romantic rendezvous at the Hilton with my wife, whom I hadn't seen in a whole month. She had arrived from Geneva a day before me. We were there with another couple, and for a whole week, we had toured about town.

The lobby and reception of the New York Hilton was no different than the street outside. It seemed like there were hundreds of people in line to check in, check out, use the elevator or use the washroom. After waiting an eternity, we finished checking out and left the desk. As we were leaving, I took a glance at the bill, which gave me a shock: for some reason, we had paid more than our friends, the other couple! They had stayed in a standard double room and so had we. They had stayed seven nights, and so had we… So why the discrepancy? I wanted to go back and ask, but we'd probably miss our flight by the time my turn in line would come. Luckily, I immediately found the assistant manager, showed him both bills and asked the reason for the difference.

"Sir, the madame was in a single room, while your friends were in a double. After the second night, the madame hosted a guest in her room," he said in what passed for an explanation.

"Whoa there! This guest you speak of is me, her husband of 22 years!" I cried.

"Sir, I have no idea who she hosted, I'm just telling you what's on the bill," he countered. "Based on a report from the cleaning staff, a surcharge for an extra bed was applied to the madame's room, resulting in the price of the room exceeding the price of the double. That's the long and the short of it."

It was clear that, for whatever reason, they had accidentally counted our room as a "single." When I came, I had assumed that the details had been taken care of, but this was evidently what happened when I didn't expressly check myself in. As it is, my wife had told me that the bathroom was dirty when she first arrived, so I reamed out the cleaner on the floor as soon as I got there – in all likelihood, the present case of affairs was probably his way of getting even!

When our son moved to New York, he – like a lot of residents – was living in a one bedroom in the city. That meant that during every one of our visits there, we were forced to shuttle from hotel to hotel: There were stays at the Waldorf Astoria, Intercontinental, The Roosevelt, Doral Tuscany, Carlyle, Gramercy Park, The Sheraton and the Aka Residences – and those are just the ones I remember. When our son finally got married and moved into a bigger house, we were freed from the rigmarole of having to stay in hotels. As for me, I was freed from the unbecoming situation of being the man secretly slipping into a woman's room…

During our week at the New York Hilton, one of the places we dined at was the Oak Room at the nearby Plaza Hotel. This restaurant/bar, which boasted wood-paneled walls, was a place that I loved and frequented until just a few years ago. The thing I liked the most about it was its ambience and quality of customers. The waiters were a bit pretentious due to all the films that were shot there, although they were still polite. They would always serve you without talking your ear off, and the food was also good. My only complaint was the small amount of gin or vodka in the G&T or Bloody Mary that I had as an apéro (or that the amount of tonic or tomato juice and ice was more than necessary).
After the Plaza Hotel was renovated, I went back to the Oak Room, but the same ambience was not to be found.
But I do wonder, does the New York Hilton still have the same atmosphere? More to the point, I would be lying if I said I didn't wonder about secretly slipping into my lover's room to get the Casanova treatment – I'd even be willing to pay the extra price!
Unfortunately, you don't get the chance to make hotel reservations like you used to – they manage to figure everything out without any mistakes these days.

It's all enough to make you wonder, where are the good ol' days?

# The Bentley At The Door Of The Poggio

## Poggio, Sausalito (California)

When they were young, my parents were great equestrians and skiers. I've always loved the pictures of them riding horses in the snow – it's as if it's a scene out of Doctor Zhivago.

My son, daughter-in-law and grandchildren all ski and play watersports.

As for me, I only go for walks.

One may infer I didn't do any sports when I was younger, but I was involved in athletics and skiing. When I was at boarding school, I signed up for the track team. But don't assume I did this out of a love for athletics – I did this so that I could leave school come evenings, as athletes at the boarding school were given permission to leave school property to train. Seizing the opportunity, my friends and I signed up for the athletics team; in time, we didn't prove ourselves to be particularly successful athletes, but we did succeed in becoming respected patrons of the meyhanes in the vicinity.

Twice I had the chance (or, more appropriately, obligation) to participate in races, representing our school in inter-school competition in cross country. The result? I abandoned one race half-way through and finished last in the other.

In the former, the race was 3,000 meters. It was cold like you wouldn't believe and there was a mix of rain and snow. We were running on the city streets; as I was bringing up the rear of the pack, a black Cadillac pulled up alongside and opened its window. Out popped the head of a quite famous actress who said:

"Come on tiger, keep it up...keep it up!" as if she was calling out to her lover coyly in a film.

The famous actress was the girlfriend of the chairman of our sports club. On that cold Sunday, she had come with her boyfriend to cheer us on, and it was from within the warm confines of her Cadillac that she encouraged me to "keep it up." The cold I was feeling soon gave way to shivers, and it seemed as if my breath was about to be taken away. When the car was out of sight, I threw in the towel – but began running faster with the intent of getting home to have some hot tea.

In the second race, I managed to finish the competition but came last: That was it!

The Athletics Federation had collected a few gifts from sponsors as incentives for a small number of participants. The gifts were small things that the firms wanting to promote their name had provided, reflecting their sector of work, and because there were enough to go around, I got one too. I didn't win a plane ticket as first place did or a weekend getaway at a hotel as second place did; instead, I got an ashtray. Personally receiving the gift from the hand of the Athletics Federation Chair was an honor I could never forget – as was the fact that they were giving an ashtray to stub out cigarettes to a high school runner!

As for skiing, my father forced me to go skiing and ice-skating a few times when I was in elementary school. Many years later, my wife and I went up the mountains one day; informing her that I knew how to ski, we put on our rented skis, got on the chairlift, and headed for the peak. Now, if I may digress, let me say that in my capacity as someone who has been happily married for 43 years, one of the keys to a happy marriage is that wives trust their husbands – on one condition: that the husband be someone to deserve that trust!

After getting off the chairlift, I attempted to take a few steps forward in preparation for showing my wife how to ski, only to discover, to my horror, that I had entirely forgotten the things I had learned about skiing when I was a child. Try as I might to move forward, the skis wouldn't budge an inch – which was probably for the best, as who knows what would have happened to us and what trouble we would have caused. As far as I can remember, they brought us down on a snowmobile. It's easy to head to the peak – so long as you don't make a fool of yourself on the way down...

Even heading up to the mountain to ski was a fiasco all on its own. I'm not particularly keen on relating it lest I really destroy any confidence you have in me, but what I did doesn't deserve to go untold. We chugged up the mountain in foggy weather with a massive, eight-cylinder American car that threatened to overheat on every hill, all without the aid of any snow tires or chains. I have no idea how we conjured up such a miracle, but cast such thoughts out of your mind: I don't want you to think ill of me.
Perhaps my only apology would be this: When we did all of this, we were 27!

My parents did different things, so did our grandchildren, and so did we.
Everyone's choices, joys, expectations and opportunities are different.
And like every subject, this is also the case in terms of food and drink. Some enjoy their meat rare, and some enjoy it well-done. Some like their pasta al dente, and some hate it this way.
That's why people who write restaurant reviews have such a difficult job, as it's technically impossible to provide a review that will embrace everyone.

One sunny June afternoon, I was in Sausalito, walking along the seashore, when I began to think about where to go for food. I could retrace a few steps and head to Scoma's on the water for fish. Or I could go forward a bit and sample some of Sushi Ran's successful Japanese fare. Then there was Napa Valley Burger Co. just over there, where, if I could find a seat, I could wolf down one of the most delectable burgers around alongside an ice-cold beer. As I pondered my course of action, a brand-new Bentley convertible glided past me like a swan, stopping in front of the Trattoria Poggio on the other side of the street. A 60-year-old with graying hair along the sides emerged from the vehicle. (What was left of his hair was probably dyed because, as far as I remember, the hair that remained on my head at that age was already white.) He was bedecked in a dark-blue cotton blazer and white pants. And with a silk shirt, sand shoes and a handkerchief, it was as if he was an Italian film producer. Instead of LA, or perhaps because he had gotten sick of LA, it seemed he had found his way north to San Francisco. Regardless, he didn't look like he was from around there. Around there, the rich winemakers of Napa Valley and the rich thinkers of Silicon Valley tend to dress in plain, comfortable attire.

The man entered the trattoria – and yours truly in his wake! He had some linguine and a glass of red wine before lighting a cigar over a glass of liquor. It was obvious to all that he was pleased with what he had consumed. As for me, I had some grilled sea bass accompanied by a glass of white wine. But if you want the truth, I was less than pleased.

If both of us were food critics, you'd be reading diametrically opposed reviews about the same restaurant. That's because people's palates, pleasures and expectations are different. Some like French cuisine with heavy sauce, while others go vegan. Some like to grace ostentatious and flashy restaurants, while some prefer a bohemian atmosphere.

And one can also add the prejudices and personal preferences of the critic on top of the difficulties that are part and parcel of producing a review that will encompass the different preferences of readers.

Critics receive special treatment at a lot of restaurants while being shown the best. Sometimes they don't have to pay the bill, sometimes you're treated to plenty of extras on the house.

In response to such attention, most critics tend to rate the restaurant in question much more highly that warranted.

In blogs, chefs, as well as food and kitchen product vendors, tend to have pride of place. But advertisers and sponsors tend to show their influence not just in blog posts but also in assorted "best restaurant" competitions.

As for restaurants, they can't possibly make the same food at the same quality every day. The chef will follow the recipe in one way, but his or her assistant will do so in a different way when the boss is away – a phenomenon that is more pronounced for chefs with different restaurants in various locales.

As far as I'm concerned, the fundamental quality that needs to be presented to the reader is the critic's honesty and independence.

Like everyone, critics have subjective views – but if they act honestly and independently, this subjectivity will be reflected objectively to the reader, instead of leading them astray or manipulating them!

" In the former, the race was 3,000 meters. It was cold like you wouldn't believe and there was a mix of rain and snow. We were running on the city streets; as I was bringing up the rear of the pack, a black Cadillac pulled up alongside and opened its window. Out popped the head of a quite famous actress who said: "Come on tiger, keep it up...keep it up" as if she was calling out to her lover coyly in a film. "

# Missing The Sunset
# At Da Gelsomina

## Da Gelsomina, Capri

Have you ever seen an Italian person that doesn't talk much? I sure haven't.

One typical Italian, i.e., one who talks a lot, succeeded in preventing my wife and me from beholding Capri's breathtaking sunset.

The Bay of Naples didn't just get famous for the Amalfi coasts, its islands and its volcano. Here, the sunset over the boundless, deep-blue sea has no equal.

We had made reservations at a restaurant called Da Gelsomina. The place is really far from Anacapri, but it is possible to get there by car after passing the countless vineyards, gardens and empty expanses. As we were making the reservation, we asked how to get there. "We'll pick you up," they said.

The restaurant is one of the places to be for the sunset. "The sun sets at 8; be ready at 7.30 because the road takes about 15 to 20 minutes," they said. Punctually, they showed up at the designated time to pick my wife and me up with a minibus. We were in high spirits. A couple of minutes after setting off, however, the minibus stopped.

"Why have we stopped?" we asked.

"We're going to pick some people up from here," the driver responded.

We waited for those special newcomers for another five minutes. In the end, they weren't that late. Four or five middle-aged Italian men boarded, offering us a "buona sera" as they filled the minibus. The restaurant said they were going to send a special vehicle just for us, but given that this is Italy, we were neither surprised nor particularly perturbed by the unscheduled development. We exited the town after a kilometer or two and began passing the vineyards until we were confronted by a car coming in the opposite direction. Because the road was narrow, we stopped to let it pass — or that's at least what we thought. Of course, wouldn't the two drivers choose this time to start a chat as the two pulled up to each other? It appeared the pair hadn't seen each other in a while and embarked on a conversation that included pleasantries along the lines of "How's Fabio and what's Claudia up to?" Just then, those in the vehicle suddenly waded into the fray, exploding in a riot of chatter as if they had known the two drivers for the past 40 years. So it commenced, and given that those in question were Italian, they weren't able to stop...

By the time we got to the restaurant, the sun had set!

I asked for some wine immediately... We began to gulp down our wine, having to settle for the residual crimson hue visible above the water. Soon the waiter arrived to take our order for food. But who might it be but the driver that had just brought us!
"You were squawking for two hours on the road; you made us miss the sunset!" I told him angrily.
Not to be outdone, he turned the tables:

"Signore, forget about the sunset, look at the one that's shining radiantly next to you."

The comment incited subordination in our team, as half of us crossed the divide to the waiter's side:
"Really, my love, what's the matter? Did we not see a sunset in Capri at all? Just let it go tonight; don't get mad at the boy!" the defector said.
As the remaining half of the split team, I retreated to the comfort of the velvet-like smoothness of my Tuscan wine, humming La Donna è Mobile to myself.

Da Gelsomina is a family restaurant perched above a cliff in a rural area of Capri. It also has a swimming pool, and people using the pool by day also dine here. Some, however, also come just for the restaurant in the evening. As I noted, the road is not particularly short, taking about 15-20 minutes by car – provided the driver doesn't get lost in conversation with someone else along the way. Ultimately, though, the road is worth it. With its garden, hall, spectacular view, delectable fare and upmarket diner profile, Da Gelsomina offers enjoyment. The restaurant is especially first rate in its raw seafood and crustaceans. Everything we had was great, but the raw red shrimp (gambero rosso) carpaccio in a balsamic sauce in a bed of garden cress and arugula salad was a masterpiece!

On the way back, a different driver took us back to our hotel. This time, there were no apologies or flattery – he returned us to the hotel promptly.
Along the way, I only learned from him about when Vesuvius erupted, the resulting ramifications, the triumphs from the days when Maradona played for Napoli, the must-see places along the Amalfi coast, the history of the restaurant, the way that Capri's population drops in winter, the seriousness of the air pollution caused by motorcycles and ferries, as well as Peppino di Capri's house – all in full detail, of course.
Ask whatever you want – I can give you an answer!

# The Women's Hamam

Solbar, Napa Valley

Before shower units made an appearance in our country, people used to go to the neighborhood bathhouse (hamam). I recall going once or twice myself. The hamam, according to my rather hazy recollection – and thus relying more on what my grandmother and grandfather related to me – is a place like this:

First, you head into a small separate room, disrobe and wrap yourself in a waistcloth provided by the hamam before donning bath clogs on your feet. Unlike the gym, you don't have to change your clothes in front of everyone!

Afterward, you head to the main section, a place that is hot, steamy, damp and bedecked in marble. Right in the middle is an altar-like stone called a "göbektaşı" under a small dome. Some choose to lie down here and sweat out their toxins for a good 15-20 minutes, while others head straight for the basin to wash.

A functionary known as a "tellak" soon comes to attend to those lying on the göbektaşı; first he administers a foam bath before scrubbing them down with a coarse bath glove. Doing so does wonders for one's pores and results in truly healthy-looking skin.

After the completion of all the scrubbing and the washing, it's out of the main section and into a hall set at a normal temperature for some resting and relaxation accompanied by tea, coffee and other beverages. The only thing then left is to return to your room, get dressed and depart.

In the past, however, the Turkish hamam had far more uses than simply, as its name suggests, being a place to bathe.

The local hamam was a place to go to for all and sundry from the neighborhood, with separate days for women and men.

The women's hamam was always full of color and fun. Because there were no cafés or restaurants in which they could meet and chat at the time, they used to get together at the hamam. Sometimes, they would pack along food as if they were going on a picnic, take along their saz, get clean and then dance while eating, drinking, singing and making merry. When viewed from this angle, the women's hamam was a much-loved place of socialization.

Such hamams were equally a place to scope out possible brides for the men in the family. With most women in those days blanketed in the chador, the women in the man's family could only cast their eye on girls betrothed to their menfolk at the hamam while they were in the nude to determine any possible bodily imperfections. For this, there was a ritual: After stripping naked, the bride-to-be would circumambulate the göbektaşı three times with her equally naked friends and accompanying relatives. The prospective groom's women relatives would sit on the göbektaşı, performing the necessary inspections. After completing the triple tour, the expectant bride would kiss the hands of her beloved's matriarchs, thus bringing the ceremony to a close and ushering in the requisite song and dance.

Additionally, the women's hamam was the spa of yesteryear, functioning as the address for epilation with various herbs, oil massages, proper scrub-downs to renew the skin, foam baths and even hair care.
Up to a certain age, boys could accompany their mothers, but when the child got a bit older, it was customary for the mother to receive a warning from the other women: "Madame... Madame... Your son's grown as big as a post, but you're still bringing him here. Maybe it's time for his dad to bring him!" Such a warning was accompanied by a cascade of erotic laughter, while the boy, left shamefaced, would no longer come, heading subsequently for the men's section along with his father.

The women's hamam also attracted plenty of attention from Orientalist writers and painters. No doubt you've seen or read about old gravures and paintings depicting how a wealthy woman and assorted concubines would wash and get clean. There's no need to mention that in these exaggerated pictures and depictions, both the customer and the people washing her were always young, beautiful and half-naked.

All of this came to mind one sunny Sunday as I was dining at Solage's Solbar. Seated in the vicinity of our table were young and well-manicured ladies sporting white bathrobes. But with their uncovered feet and the way their bathrobes spread when they crossed their legs, the image created certainly didn't fall short of the erotic ones depicted by Orientalist painters from the Turkish women's hamam. What's more, these women hadn't even gone for a swim in the pool in front of us. So why on earth were they sitting in bathrobes?

My son was on hand to satisfy my curiosity: "These are all women who've come from Solage's Spa."
I really like the hotel-restaurants that appear before you when you get out of San Francisco. Particularly on Sunday afternoons, they offer a wonderful chance to eat in peace in a beautiful and well-maintained garden. But I like Solage and its Solbar even more.

And if you're wondering what I dined on at its restaurant, which is recommended by Michelin, I'm not going to say, "I couldn't remember because I kept on looking around me." As it is, I gazed around intently. These young ladies, who come to the spa to get fit, mostly dug into double cheeseburgers, French fries and giant sandwiches – just like Turkish women at the hamam!
As for me, I contented myself with grilled chicken and a few glasses of wine.

# The Benefits
# Of Walking

## La Pergola, Rome

The Rome Cavalieri Hotel is quite far from the city center. That's why its lobby and garden aren't filled with curious tourists who just drop by to see the interior. You have to be a serious walker like me to come here on foot. Actually, I wasn't a disciplined walker even though I love walking, but that was only until my son got me a Fitbit. You record the number of steps you want to take every day into this watch-like device, which vibrates when you've reached your goal. Ever since I started using the contraption, I've walked with great discipline until it vibrates and, as if it's a legal requirement, don't go to bed unless it does so. My daily goal is 10 thousand steps; when I reach this number, my Fitbit vibrates and lets me know. Most of the time I reach 12-13 thousand steps. I even make it to 18-19 thousand in cities where it's impossible to get a cab or drive, like Rome.

The distant and serene Cavalieri is my favorite hotel. I especially like its lobby. It's almost like an art gallery with its giant paintings, carpets on the walls, statues and antique furniture. Even the reception desk is a real work of art. Some hotels love exhibiting artworks such as the Capri Palace in Capri and the Gramercy Park Hotel in New York. But none of them have as rich a collection as the Cavalieri. The stands that are sometimes set up on the ground floor of the main foyer – where this rich and expensive collection is displayed – are the only things that disrupt the panorama. The small stands that resemble street vendors' pushcarts really don't go well here.

I also like the garden where the lions run. It's not that big but it gives you peace with the greenery that they maintain all through the year.

The poolside offers great entertainment even though hotel customers don't usually come to the pool. People who come to Rome usually tour the city or engage in business dealings. This pool, meanwhile, is the place for Rome's rich and beautiful. It's fun to sit at the pool bar and watch them flirt while eating amazing ice cream... I don't like the ice cream in Rome even though it's very famous – for me, it's just a cream bomb. But this is not the case at the pool bar at the Cavalieri, as it's homemade and really good, especially the mint.

Another famous spot at the hotel is the La Pergola restaurant on the top floor. It has three Michelin stars and has managed to protect its privileged status for many years. The food and service deserve these three stars. It has a very extensive wine cellar but what surprised me was the rich selection of water. If I'm not mistaken, the menu offered 30-40 different types of water.

In the end, when you're dining in Italy, they look down on you if you don't order pasta. Since we were aware of this fact, we ordered pasta to avoid being labeled as "out of towners." For starters, my wife ordered duck tortellini and I ordered cacio e pepe. Hers was great while mine was a little heavy. My wife cooks this at home without pecorino Romano and parmigiano but instead with lean and unsalted cheeses, making it lighter.

The pigeon and lobster we had later on were perfect. At the same time, I don't think there's much to say about a cheese platter in Italy. When you set foot in La Pergola, you first notice the paintings, carpets, candelabrum and porcelain, all of which strike you as magnificent. Your admiration hits the top when you look to your right and see the view, which offers a take on the entire city. I don't think there is a woman in the world that a man couldn't impress with a candlelight dinner on the terrace of this restaurant – as long as he has the cash. Because while he is admiring the city and muttering "Wow, the Coliseum" and "Wow, the Pantheon," when the time comes to pay up, he can only say: "Wow, the check!"

Of course, the check is high enough here to make you say "wow." This may not mean much to rich seniors or people with access to the company account, but other mere mortals might have to tell the object of their desire:

"What do you think about walking back after this amazing dinner for the sake of digestion, amore?"

And that's because you might want to skip paying for a cab on top of the huge bill; that's when you realize the benefits of being able to walk long distances. The next day you might even get a Fitbit!

...To become a more disciplined, stronger walker!

# If You're Going To Do A Job, Do It Right

## Chez Janou, Paris

If you're going to do a job, do it right, or don't do it at all.

I graduated from law school with honors. I had many alternatives before me: I could be a lawyer, judge or prosecutor or continue with an academic career. In order to make the right choice, I pondered my options and also consulted people whose wit and expertise I trusted. One of them was a famous law professor, a friend of my family, who also practiced law. One day, he invited me home, offering me coffee when I arrived. After polishing off my cup, I broached the subject, soliciting his opinion and advice. He thought for a while, mentioned a name and asked me if I knew him. I did. He was a clarinet master. Unfortunately, he didn't play classical music but popular songs – a type of music that didn't have a place in our Jacobin world. I didn't know how to respond. If I told the professor that I recognized the name, he might say that I wouldn't be able to make it to the top if I listened to such drivel. And if I told him that I didn't know the name, he might say that I didn't know what was going on in the world and that I would fail in whichever profession I selected. When he sensed my hesitation, he said:

"Look, I won't tell you which profession to choose, but I will give you more important advice: This man plays popular songs in taverns and at weddings. You might look down on him. But that would be a mistake because no matter where this guy plays, he is good at what he does; he is a star in his profession. So, in whichever profession you pick, you need to do it to the best of your abilities. This is the secret to success."

I never forgot this basic advice and have always tried to follow it: If you put your mind to doing something, you have to do your best!

The purpose of restaurants is to make people go out and eat outside. In order to achieve this purpose, they need to offer tasty food, various beverages, knowledgeable and warm service, a décor that pleases people and an agreeable price. This is what is expected from them. If they can't provide these, why would anyone go to a restaurant? Every restaurant tries to offer something unique to draw customers.

Chez Janou is one of these restaurants. It's a cute bistro in the intellectual/bohemian Parisian quarter of Marais. Basically, it's a restaurant that serves pastis in a country of wine. If you look at the walls and the menu, you can see that they offer all kinds of pastis, which is a liquor containing aniseed. At least that's what you'd think. I asked the waiter for Turkish rakı, which, as encyclopedias suggest, is a distilled Turkish drink with aniseed that is quite strong. That is why it's best consumed as an aperitif, except in Turkey, where people consume it with a meal. I think the best rakı is produced in Turkey, with my favorite being the Yeni Rakı Yeni Seri. It's probably not the most refined rakı in comparison with some, but it's the one that best suits my pallet.

Since it's strong, it's consumed slowly, which fosters both long conversation and the healthy consumption of food. Isn't meeting with friends and enjoying long conversations one of the reasons people go to restaurants?

I couldn't find it on the menu of Chez Janou but there was one called "Raki Turque," so I ordered that out of desperation. The waiter brought one, a rakı made in Marseilles. Judging by the name and the place of manufacture, the producer was probably an Armenian from Turkey. It wasn't all that bad. I ordered a few different types of rakı from the menu and tried them one by one, including Hanri Louis Pernod, Lou Castellanou and Pastis de Provence. All three were interesting. However, a restaurant that boasts over 80 types of pastis but couldn't offer a single one from its country of origin gets a minus from me. The walls, shelves and menu were filled with various types of rakı, but the most famous ones didn't exist! I don't know if this was an oversight or a conscious choice. And I didn't have to know.

Instead, I remembered the advice the professor had given me about doing your job to the best of your abilities…

I had one last drink and toasted his health!

# On What Married Women Suffer From The Language Of Men

## Carlton Beach, Cannes

Here's an open secret:

Men chase after women, beg and plead, convince them to marry them with a thousand and one methods of flattery and then – after the wedding – subject them to every manner of verbal tribulation imaginable. Why is this? Billions of inkwells have probably run dry trying to explain the reason. What's clear is that many, many more will run dry trying to explain this state of affairs in the time to come as well.

Instead of embarking upon an analysis of the union of men and women – a task surely more difficult than splitting the atom – let me relate an unseemly comparison that I recently heard.

This guy (name unknown) said this:

"A married woman is like a TV, while a girlfriend is like a mobile phone.

"You watch TV at home; when you go out, you carry your mobile with you.

"A TV is free for life, but your mobile is cut off as soon as you fail to pay the bill.

"Speaking on a mobile is two-way – you talk and you listen. With a TV, however, all you do is listen."

Where did this gauche comparison come from, you ask? From the couple eating at the next table over! Given the man's exaggerated interest, it was clear that the woman sitting across the table was, within the parameters of the aforementioned tactless description, a "mobile phone" – although a phone of decidedly old and unwieldy provenance. From her head to the sandals on her feet, she was glistening gaudily in a dress sporting much embroidery. Her phone case was even like that. Where on earth would she wear such elaborate evening attire?

To the beach restaurant of the Carlton Hotel!

The Carlton is an icon of Cannes and one of the first things to come to mind when one mentions the city. During the annual film festival, famous artists and cinema people spend the night there. Still, for all its reputation, it's a hotel that has become fairly ratty and antiquated. This is something that becomes apparent as soon as you enter the lobby. The sitting room is filled with old (not classic) furniture and coffee tables. The windows, meanwhile, are covered with tulle curtains. We weren't up for eating there, so we crossed over to the restaurant on the seafront opposite the hotel.

And it's a good thing we did: We had come to a beach restaurant that was much more dynamic with better service and more satisfying fare. On a warm autumn day next to the sea, we sampled some farmed sea bass that wasn't half-bad. I asked, and they said it had come from Corsica, and it cost significantly less than the same sea bass we had had at the Eden Roc. To be frank, they didn't provide a fish knife, but I'm not sure if paying 20 euros more for the same fish just for the privilege of using a fish knife is a sound investment. The grilled vegetables served alongside the fish were themselves colorful, vivid and delectable. The same went for the salad that was crowned with fennel, and we enthusiastically ate everything with the accompaniment of white wine.

While gazing off at those lying on the perfect sand by the water, my wife asked:
"Are you happy with your new mobile?"
I was instantly startled. If I had been young, I would have looked into her eyes and tried to determine whether there was something between the lines of her question.
"I'm happy, although it doesn't get reception everywhere," I said, choosing my words carefully.
"Don't forget it!"
"I won't," I said, taking it from the table and inserting it into the pocket of my trousers with care.

At the next table, the man with dyed hair was continuing his barrage of compliments to the iridescent woman. We got up, and started walking hand in hand along the Croisette.

Single men, I guarantee that if you choose a good TV, you'll be able to watch great things your whole life! Decide for yourself on the mobile issue…. But I hope you won't forget that women never drop their mobile phones!

# The Ocean Of Anisa And Aslan

## Grill Garden, Bodrum

Anisa was born in Manhattan and lived there until she was two. She never woke up to the sound of roosters.

Her brother Aslan was born in San Francisco; he never swam in the sea when he was a baby. All he saw were a couple of courageous surfers in the cold waters of the Pacific while he played on the beach during weekends.

When they came to Bodrum for their holidays, they insisted on going to the "ocean" as soon as they woke up and put on their bathing suits.
For them, the "sea" was the "ocean;" that's all they had seen and known. It wasn't easy explaining to them that this was the Aegean Sea and the Mediterranean Sea and not an ocean.

I'm a born and bred Mediterranean.

We are still fortunate enough to be woken up by roosters, and swimming is still an enjoyable pastime.
The sun sets beautifully in the evening and the moon rises elegantly.
One of the things that makes the evening enjoyable is being able to have a couple of drinks on the shore and have long conversations as the sound of waves reverberate in your ears.

The Garden Grill within Hapimag Resort in Bodrum is one of the places that offers such enjoyment.
It's a beach restaurant. Tables are located where the sands kiss the sea. While you're swimming during the day, you can't wait for them to set up the tables for the evening. After your shower, you sit down at the table

with your meat and fish – or grill them yourself with an accompanying barbecue if you so desire – with nothing but the most genuine examples of sea and sand beneath your feet...

The opportunity for this, which you certainly won't find in New York or San Francisco, whispers in your ear that, despite all the trials and tribulations, life remains wonderful. It reminds you that true wealth is being alive!

It's up to you whether or not to believe this, or whether or not to be satisfied with this. For now, though, the meatballs are ready, so let me set Anisa and Aslan down to eat... It's time they took a break from screaming with delight as they and their friends throw morsels of bread at the fish...

# Are All The Ginas In Italy Beautiful?

## Osteria Le Logge, Siena

"No prosciutto...No formaggio...No pasta..."

That's what I (without even looking at the menu in my hand) told the waitress when she came to take my order as soon as I had sat down. "I don't want any of it!"
And why, because I don't like them?
On the contrary; I love them all. But if you stay 10 days in Italy's Emilia Romagna region and do nothing but eat such dishes from dawn till dusk, you're bound to shout an emphatic "no" to this triumvirate by the time you get to neighboring Tuscany, no matter how much you love them.

The Emilio Romagna region boasts an array of gastronomical riches, such as Parma ham, parmigiano cheese and balsamic vinegar. It's got a leg up on the market on cold cuts, cheese and dough-based concoctions, but it's a bit thin on the ground in terms of variations on seafood, stews and olive-oil dishes. Although the region's soil is quite fertile as far as fruits and vegetables are concerned, it's a tall order finding such riches on your plate.

If we'd been in France, we probably would have gotten an earful from the waitress about what, precisely, we intended to eat if we weren't interested in prosciutto, frommagio formaggio or pasta. That's not what happened here, however. Without missing a beat, the waitress began to explain the other options on the menu with a smile.
Osteria Le Logge is a restaurant I recommend in Siena – that's of course if you manage to enter Siena with a car! The heavy traffic – particularly in the summer months – narrow streets, lack of adequate parking

space and distance from the center in the old city is a serious problem. If you manage to overcome these problems and reach Le Logge, you might, like me, still declare that you "don't want this" and "don't want that" in a pique of grumpiness due to the heat and fatigue. Still, the Tuscans probably won't get angry at you either but will provide you service with a smile. And soon, you'll have forgotten all about the heat, the traffic and your fatigue as you dig into a fine meal.

After all, the residents of the Tuscan Valley might not possess the technological sophistication of their counterparts in Silicon Valley and might not invent devices to make our lives easier, but they've turned finding joy in the life they make easier into an art form.

Gianni Brunelli, who established Le Logge in 1997, is also the producer of the Brunello di Montalcino range of wines. An intriguing Tuscan, this is how he defined his approach to gastronomy when he opened the restaurant: "Food is important! It's impossible to avoid eating healthily! Dining with friends at my restaurant is a source of joy!"

It behooves one to pair Tuscany's local tastes with wonderful wines, but enriching this with hospitality needs to be the main goal. Brunelli set off on his path with this in mind, joining Christoph M. Mann in writing "Osteria Le Logge: La Cucina Toscana," which delves into the food of Tuscany.

There used to be a pharmacy in place of the restaurant; perhaps that's why the walls today are decorated with glass cupboards that used to contain medicine but are today full of bottles or wine and books.

Even the chairs for children reflect the restaurant's special personality, sporting wooden frames and seats made of straw.

Gianni, who attached great importance to providing a high quality of hospitality alongside taste, passed away in 2008. His wife, Laura, picked up the baton and has continued to pursue the same approach as defined at the start. There is not a computer in sight at the establishment, but there are books... There is no place for irritation toward customers but there is an unending supply of hospitality...

It was in such an atmosphere that I had a most enjoyable meal. I don't reckon it's necessary to relate what I ate, because you're likely to encounter another menu if you go. Let me just say that I topped off my visit with a Brunello di Montalcino Riserva produced by the Brunelli couple.

Before leaving, I got a chance to talk to the waitress, who had displayed a smile from the moment I sat down at the table to feast on Chef Nico Atrigna's wonderful creations.

"What's your name?" I asked.

"Gina."

"Dolce Gina, are all the Ginas in Italy beautiful like you?"

One of Gina's namesakes, Gina Lollobrigida, was a leading actress of the 1960s. While in Hollywood, 20th Century Film started calling her "Mona Lisa" after she played in the company's films, and not without reason, as she was a truly beautiful woman.

I thanked Gina, Nico and Mirco and departed.

It was a different meal on that night. The following night was sure to again feature a dinner starting with prosciutto, continuing with pasta and concluding with parmigiano aged to 30 months.

Accompanied, naturally, by a good Brunello di Montalcino!

# You're The Woman Of My Bed!

## Bebek Balıkçı, Istanbul

If a man says "you're the woman of my bed" to a woman, it means he chooses her, loves her and is there to protect her. If it's expressed with an erotic, romantic fashion – instead of a macho imperiousness – then I suspect that there is no woman who wouldn't be swayed by the remark.

And even if there is, she'd be the exception. One of these exceptions, however, just happens to be my wife... Occasionally, I have been known to snore. In such instances, my wife escapes to the other room. I let her have it at breakfast, though, albeit in a somewhat sheepish and guilty fashion.

"Don't leave my side... You're the woman of my bed!"

I think it's an impactful turn of phrase, but sleep is also wonderful and necessary. The poor woman is left vacillating between a wonderful turn of phrase and the necessity of sleep. When I start to snore, should she stay in bed, tossing and turning without sleeping a wink or head to the other room and get a beauty rest? Should she stay or should she go? If I have to admit it, after you hit 70, a good night's sleep carries a lot more weight than any romantic sweet nothings.

When I ask at breakfast why she went to the other room, she doesn't say, "Go to hell, you didn't let me sleep at all with all that snoring," but opts instead to say silent and give me an affectionate kiss. I consume the 40 grams of muesli, the half banana and the kefir that she has presented before me with a degree of both guilt and reproach, but I opt not to belabor the matter.

The situation at some restaurants is no different. There are aspects that you really like that entice you to come, but there are other aspects that are sure to give you pause for regret and convince you to head for the door. You're bound to be caught between two minds about whether to go or stay.

Bebek Balıkçı is that kind of restaurant.

Located at one of the most beautiful bends of the Bosphorus, the restaurants offers patrons the chance to dine on a wharf just a meter above the water. While listening to the waves lap below, diners can even hold out a rod and catch fish. And if you squeeze past the yachts that have anchored in the area, a quick swim will soon bring you to another great continent, Asia. At the same time, you're likely to deem it a great misfortune if you happen to catch a glimpse of the full moon poking out from between the groves and historical mansions on the opposite shore but aren't able to the share the moment with a loved one. As it is, that's usually the case, because most come to Bebek Balıkçı for business lunches or dinners. It's an expensive restaurant, but they take care to offer the freshest fish, and their service is good.

But as someone who has been frequenting this restaurant and the ones near it for more than half a century, one has to note that the menu is always the same: First some white cheese, melon, bonito, eggplant paste and beans in olive oil; shrimp casserole or a plate of calamari in between, and then the fish of the day. If you're going to have this just once or a few times, then that's fine – it's better than most restaurants along the Mediterranean. But, perchance, if you want to soak in the wonderful view with any frequency or you routinely want to take clients there, choosing to eat the same exact menu for years on end is likely to become a bit of a bore. As such, you might find yourself racked by indecision: To go or not to go!

Perhaps you're conservative in your tastes, or perhaps you appreciate change; extend your invitation accordingly!

# The Paradise Of Il Riccio After The Inferno Of The Marina Grande

## Il Riccio, Capri

For those going to Capri for the first time, the adventure starts at Naples' harbor.

As he drops you off, your taxi driver will indicate the general direction of a booth: "You'll get your ticket there."

It's 10.30 in the morning, and you are aware that the ferry belonging to the Caremar company that will take you to Capri leaves at 11.30. You're in the know, and the time suits you just fine. You approach the booth indicated by the driver. It's occupied. You inquire to the woman waiting in front of you:

"This is where we get the Caremar ticket to Capri, right?"

The woman hesitates for a second, inspects the notice affixed to the booth's window and returns to you:

"No, sorry, you don't get the tickets from here!" she announces.

"What!? But the taxi driver said it was here. So where are we supposed to get them from?" I plead.

"This is Porto Beverello – you have to go to Porto di Masso," she advises us.

"Where's that? Is it far?"

"Not particularly… About a kilometer away where those buildings are."

"Are you sure?"

"Of course. I'm from here."

No worries then: You've got enough time to get to the ferry, and you've got a straw hat on your head to ward off the sun. Still, in the heat of August, you set off on the road, dragging your suitcase along with you. You arrive at the appointed area to be confronted by four or five different companies that carry passengers from Naples to the islands and other locations. All of them have assorted ticket booths at the Beverello and Massa harbors. And even after securing your ticket, the pier from which you will board your boat is somewhere else. But as it is, there is no proper sign indicating how to get to the ticket sales point. Ultimately, dripping in sweat and asking everyone and their dog right, left and center, you find the Caremar ticket booth.

"Is this where you buy Caremar tickets for Capri?" you inquire.

"Si, signor."

At long last, you've finally found it – what's more, there's still half an hour until the ferry.

"Two people for the 11.30 boat, please."

"The 11.30 sailing doesn't go from here – we don't sell the ticket for that. The 14.30 goes from here; do you want tickets for that?"

"What do you mean you don't sell the ticket? Isn't this the Caremar booth?"

"It is the Caremar booth, but the 11.30 boat is a hydrofoil. We only sell ferry tickets here. The first ferry is at 14.30. Do you want that?"

Among the people of the world, the term for a sea-going vessel that transports people a short distance between Point A and Point B is a "ferry." Who on God's green earth would expect there to be both a ferry and a hydrofoil in Naples and that the sailings for each of these would be offered by four or five companies? Each company has different sales booths in the two ports separated by a kilometer, while the hydrofoil ticket isn't sold at the place that sells ferry tickets and vice versa. Then add to that the fact that the places to board the ferries are all in different locations.

"So, what should we do now?"

"If you want to go with the 14.30, I can give you tickets, but if you want to go with the 11.30 hydrofoil, then you'll need to go back to Beverello."

The scale of the disaster can be gleaned from the sweat on your head. With what remains of your strength, you mull the possibility of retracing the last kilometer to catch the ferry. With suitcases in hand in temperatures reaching 33 degrees Celsius, you chart a quick route back, find the correct booth by asking all and sundry, learn the location of the pier and make it onto the boat just as it's about to depart. As you board, those in charge have a glance at your ticket:

"You didn't get tickets for your suitcases!"

"What ticket for crying out loud? No one at the booth told us we needed to get a separate ticket for our bags. The person selling the tickets never asked us about any bags, how big they are, or what have you. What are we supposed to do now?"

There could only be one answer, naturally: "You have to go get tickets for your bags!"

The ferry is about to leave, and the ticket booth is a way's away. The next ferry is not for three hours and it leaves from a pier a full kilometer away. There are two courses of action open to you: If you pride yourself on following the rules and are left with no other options, you will miss the ferry, go get in the long queue to get a ticket for your bag, trek the one kilometer to the other port and wait three hours for the next ferry. But if, perchance, you're not one married to the rules and, more importantly, are a resourceful Mediterranean, you can solve the bag ticket problem on the spot for just a small financial outlay and board as the last passenger.

The maiden adventure to Capri generally starts like this from Naples' port!

For those going for the second or third time, I can't say that it's particularly different – just that the adventure becomes a little bit easier.

You've now learned where to get the ticket for which ferry in Naples, as well as which pier to go from, but when the matter comes to actually disembarking at Capri, you're at a loss. I don't care if you come a hundred times; trouble will never cease to dog you.

Hundreds of people with suitcases and strollers are funneling through on the narrow pier at once...
Hundreds of others, with suitcases and strollers in tow, are waiting in the exact same spot to board the emptying ferry.
It's the same spot where long queues are forming in front of the ticket booths.
Tourist groups leave from the same spot.
There are taxis, shuttles arriving for the guests of expensive hotels... and even buses dropping off and picking up passengers all in the same spot...
For those that want to head to Capri with the funicular, the queue is in the same spot.
Cafés and bars, pizzerias, gelato places, souvenir shops...
Buzzing scooters that you couldn't free yourself of even if you were to swat them like mosquitoes...
All of these are crammed into a cramped area that is not much larger than half a football pitch.
If Dante Alighieri were alive today, I reckon he'd revise the Inferno chapter of the Divine Comedy and add another section!

Those looking for respite drag themselves off to a hotel. We picked the Il Riccio...
The Il Riccio Beach Club has a restaurant with a Michelin star.
You've been worn out by the ports in Naples and Capri, so let me cut to the chase and say: It's a really good restaurant.
It overlooks the deep, dark blue waters of the Bay of Naples with a view of the Ischia and Procida islands.
It's quite unornamented but amiable with its blue tables and chairs and white tablecloths.
From the chef to the waiter, the kitchen and service team is top notch.
The antipasti, pastas, primi and secondi are all delectable...
But beware of entering the dessert salon known as the Temptation Room. There are so many enticing desserts on offer that you could enter the room totally healthy and leave it as a diabetic.
That's why capping off your meal with some limoncello and espresso might be a better idea.
But what is most wonderful about the place are the guests that turn every evening into a wedding feast.
Some even come from Sorrento and the islands by boat. Men and women, old and young – everyone sports an unassuming chic... You'll never see anyone overdoing it style-wise. No one swaggers around, and no one's looking at the other tables to see what someone else is wearing. On the contrary, everyone remains in their own happy world, eating, drinking and chatting. The peals of laughter don't advance beyond the table. Naturally, there are mass toasts every 10 minutes and many warm embraces between men and women.
A warm Mediterranean atmosphere like this absolutely relaxes and enthuses any onlooker, bringing them into the fold. There's such a joyful atmosphere that even if the food weren't that great, you'd be bound to reckon it's some of the best in the world. Of course, there are no such worries here, as the lobster, octopus and pezzogna and everything else presented here is fantastic. When I asked for a pen and paper to jot down the Italian names of what I had, they returned with a printed menu of what I ate: What could that be but the height of elegance!

Humans possess two characteristics that keep them going when faced with adversity: forgetting and hoping.
Forget about the tribulations at the ports in Naples and Capri, imagine the pleasure awaiting you at Il Riccio and go.

You won't regret it!

> **If Dante Alighieri was alive today, I reckon he'd revise the Inferno chapter of the Divine Comedy and add another section!**

# Dinner By Heston Blumenthal And La Bohème

## Dinner By Heston Blumenthal, London

On the last night of 1985, we rang in the New Year at London's Hyde Park Hotel.

It was one of the most prestigious hotels in London. The rooms are decorated in a traditional style, and I'll never forget the tub that was as big as a bathroom located right in the center. The hotel later changed hands, and even if the façade remained the same, the interior was subjected to an extensive modernization. The breakfast room (which doubled as the main dining hall) looked out onto Hyde Park. Similarly to all big old hotels, it was large. The tables were spaced out from each other and draped in linen, while the waiters served you with gloves on.

On our New Year's Eve, we were serenaded to our room with the sound of bagpipes; it was the first time we had heard a piper in a kilt play the bagpipes. We were surprised, but we liked the sound.
The day after, there was something that surprised and pleased me even more when we came down for breakfast: fruit.

We stood gaping at the fruit in the magnificent hall, which looked onto the expanse of green in Hyde Park. The fruit plate looked like a Naturmort from the hand of an accomplished painter. This fruit wasn't like what we have there. I was struck most by the strawberries – they were enormous. We couldn't bring ourselves to eat or even touch the fruit. I guess it meant that in a luxury hotel in Britain, they ate fruits that were a lot different than what we had. Is this the difference wealth makes? We thought it unfortunate that we didn't have something like this back home.

Years passed… We finally put two and two together that the fruit basket that we had spied enviously actually consisted of genetically modified concoctions full of hormones. At the time, this scourge hadn't yet reached our shores. First the scourge infected the advanced nations, but while the rich were digging into opulent but hormone-filled food in England, we were enjoying our gnarled and crooked – but natural – fruit! Thirty years went by – this time we didn't come to the hotel to stay for the night, but to eat.
The hotel's name had changed; it was now the Mandarin Oriental.

The dining hall had also changed; the wide and large hall had been partitioned into smaller areas, meaning that it no longer possessed that overpowering grandiosity.

The sober decoration of before had been replaced by a modern interior design featuring wood, leather, iron and glass.

The tables draped with linen had given way to bare tables.
Even the waiters' attire had changed; gone were the white uniforms and the older waiters who wore them, to be replaced by young men and women in everyday dress.

In his song La Bohème, Charles Aznavour relates how he has come to the realization about how happy he was when he would just get enough to fill his stomach in exchange for a picture in the cafés of Montmartre. But when he returns to the same haunts, he notes, with melancholy, that "Montmartre is not the same as it was before. Everything's changed, and I don't recognize the streets and houses. Even the color of the lilacs has faded away."

I felt the same sense of alienation when I returned to the Mandarin's dining hall. Feeling a wave of melancholy, I saw that nothing was as I had left it.

But the sadness I had felt at the entrance began to dissipate after I sat down at my table.
The name of the dining hall had been given to someone famous: Heston Blumenthal.

It's true; the passage of time doesn't make everything worse. In fact, perhaps we're not searching for the quality of the past when "casting our mind back," but our "youth that remains in the past"… Who knows? We were treated to a crescendo of delight from the moment we sat down at Dinner by Heston Blumenthal until the moment we rose to depart.

The servers were young men and women who always presented a smiling face, knew their jobs well and never allowed any delays in service thanks to their distant but continuous observation of the table, all while ensuring that their service was not overbearing for the customer.

When I invited the sommelier to the table, I'd be lying if I said I didn't think to myself, "What does this person know about this job?" when I saw that it was a young lady. I quickly felt ashamed, however, when sipping one of the wines she paired with our food. The 2010 New Zealand Syrah from the Craggy Range Gimblett Gravels Vineyard that she recommended to us left us enraptured.

As for the food, one can only define the meal presented by Heston Blumenthal, one of the world's most famous chefs, and the executive chef Ashley Palmer-Watts as a "work of art."

Blumenthal is the owner and chef of the famous Fat Duck. Everything started with the interest he began showing in French cuisine when he joined his family on a trip to France at the age of 16. This was followed by the years in which he honed his skills. I don't think it would be an overstatement to categorize the subsequent phase as one in which Heston "developed cuisine." His approach to food is scientific, and he is one of the pioneers of molecular gastronomy. He takes different foods and combines them with unique techniques to create completely new inventions, like white chocolate caviar and ice cream with bacon and eggs. He researches, he works, he writes books, he makes TV programs, he gives conferences... At the end of the day, he's a kitchen engineer that stands before you with honorary doctorates from two universities, Reading and London. The Fat Duck and Dinner by Heston Blumenthal are duly regarded as two of the world's best restaurants. The first boasts three Michelin macaroons, while the other sports two.

I'm not much of a fan of molecular gastronomy products on principle, but I can do nothing but doff my cap at the food created by Blumenthal following his research of 15th- and 16th-century English cuisine, as each of our dishes was more delicious than the next. The cold lobster soup made with the water of a cucumber and a classic dish called meat fruit stood out the most among the starters. As for mains, the duck, which was squeezed into powder, was exquisite. The rare Filet Mignon was cooked in the way they instruct future chefs to do so at the Cordon Bleu – such that they were as pink as can be but produced not a gram of blood when cut. For the spicy pigeon, however, I can't even find the words. If I say "beyond extraordinary," it might just capture some of the taste.

And finally there were the strawberries in the Spring Tart. They weren't like the huge and garish berries I had eaten in the same hall 30 years ago; instead, they were small with excellent scent and taste.
It means that not everything goes bad with age!

Without question, Dinner by Heston Blumenthal is now on my list of favorite restaurants.

> 66 On our new Year's Eve, we were serenaded to our room with the sound of bagpipes; it was the first time we had heard a piper in a kilt play the bagpipes. We were surprised, but we liked the sound. The day after, there was something that surprised and pleased me even more when we came down for breakfast; fruit. 99

# I Wasn't Cut Out To Be A Violinist

## Na Cosu, Belgrade

Na Coşu is a small and elegant restaurant in Belgrade.

Contrary to other restaurants in the city, such as Dva Jelena, it doesn't have a local character. When you're dining there, you won't be able to hear Balkan sounds like in restaurants on Skadarlija Street. It doesn't have the futuristic feel of Lorenzo i Kakalamba. It mostly reminds you of La Belle Époque French bistros.

When we went to Belgrade for two years because of my father's job, I was just 11 years old. They enrolled me in a school that also drew diplomats' children. If someone in my co-ed class misbehaved, the British teachers would enforce the "underwear" punishment, which entailed spanking the kid on the bottom after removing their underwear. Either they didn't know that such punishment was a huge blow to the psyche of the kid on the receiving end, or this type of punishment was part of the education system in England at that time. I can honestly say that I didn't learn anything tangible at the school. In fact, I guess the purpose wasn't to teach kids anything but to subjugate them. There were no shared values, joys or pains that the children from different countries could share, except for one.

When I got to school one Monday morning, I saw that all the children were upset and that the British kids were crying. I asked around and found out that the plane of Man Utd, who had just played a match against the Yugoslavian team Crvena Zvezda (Red Star) in Belgrade, had gone down while taking off in Munich. This made me sadder than the other kids because I had seen the game the other day with my father at Partizan Stadium. The game finished 3-3, which put Manchester United into the semi-final of the European Cup. Sadly, however, there was now no one to play in the semi-final!

I have often witnessed joy and unhappiness arrive at the same time. I don't know if this is a coincidence or the natural flow of life. One thing I do know is that I've been a supporter of Manchester United ever since. Besides school, my sister and I got French lessons from two spinsters. There was an ice-skating rink on Taşmegdan near our house and we used to skate there. My sister also took ballet lessons. When my father's post ended and we were about to leave Belgrade, her teachers said she had great talent and that they would make her a world-class ballerina if she stayed in Belgrade. However, it wasn't an option to leave an 8-year-old girl there, meaning that she missed the chance to become a famous ballerina, although she did become a professor of political science!

As for me, my father had bought me a violin and hired a young and beautiful teacher from the conservatory. Intriguingly, my father had wanted his kids to become violinists. Previously, he'd bought a violin for my brother when we was little, but he, unfortunately, also failed to become a violinist, although he did become a professor of constitutional law. At that time, the most famous violinist was Yascha Heifetz. My father hoped that I would also become a virtuoso like him one day and even called me "Hayfez." My first lessons went great; lessons that dealt with how to hold the violin and the bow and where the fingers went were easy. But when it came time to play by looking at the notes, that young and beautiful teacher of mine turned into a witch who would brandish a broom in front of my eyes. I began to sneak off to my friends, pretending that I'd forgotten about my lessons. My father realized the situation in no time and ended the lessons.

Years passed, until he said during a conversation over drinks:
"We hired you an 18-year-old fox and even then you couldn't deal with this violin stuff!" At the time, I was going through Andropause, so I shot back:
"But daddy, I was just 11 years old at that time. Now you hire me an 18-year-old fox and watch me tackle that violin!"

"But daddy, I was just 11 years
old at that time. Now you hire me an
18-year-old fox and watch
me tackle that violin".

# A Tasting Menu Is Like A Fashion Show

## Zelmira, Modena

The attire on display at a fashion show is generally not the kind you can wear pretty much anywhere; instead, it's pretty over the top. Fashion designers pull out the stops to show off their creativity. As you watch, the dresses pass you by in a blur...

Tasting menus also tend to be designed to showcase the craft and ingenuity of the chef. Whether you like it or not, seven or eight items of food are presented before you in succession. Like what you sample? Too bad, that's all there is. If you don't, then you just sit and watch.

I'm not a fan of tasting menus at all. If there's nothing I'm particularly interested in, I don't go to restaurants that specialize in only one thing. I'm not a gourmet, and I don't attach much importance to witnessing the skills of the chefs. I go to eat at a restaurant with a pleasant atmosphere and good service, as well as to enjoy a good serving of conversation – a couple of spoonfuls of food is enough for me. If there's a dessert I really enjoy, the menu might extend to three spoonfuls, but that's it.

It was then that Zelmira in Modena appeared before me, promising a restaurant that seemed tailor-made for me.

We had tired ourselves out during the day, perusing the museums of Enzo Ferrari and Luciano Pavarotti.

The house that Enzo Ferrari, the father of the famous car brand, sold to purchase a race car later became a museum. Can you do anything but tip your hat to this passion and leap of faith by Enzo? His passion now continues today in the form of race cars that leave race tracks resounding in noise.

Before Luciano Pavarotti became one of our era's most famous tenors, he took a few of his first steps in opera at the Ankara State Opera – in 1960, if I recall. Strangely, they sent Pavarotti packing from the Ankara

Opera because his massive voice was deemed to be "lacking." Such a justification, however, isn't fooling anybody; even if those years were Pavarotti's first in the profession, it seems far from logical that his voice would be "lacking." Likewise, it seems far-fetched the managers of the Ankara Opera would have failed to understand a good voice when they heard it. The rumor that has since been whispered ear to ear, though, is this: The Italian took a pass at the conductor's beautiful actress wife, and that was enough for the opera to bundle him out the door.

Located 20 minutes by car from Modena, Pavarotti's domain in the final years of his life is fairly modest. It's an unostentatious house with a garden, salon, bedroom, kitchen and bathroom. When you compare it with the houses of the stars we see on the news, it's impossible not to be amazed. Perhaps the only expensive thing in the house is the maestro's piano!

By the time we arrived at Zelmira, I was still humming Nessun Dorma, an aria that the maestro Pavarotti sang in front hundreds of thousands in Central Park.

The restaurant is located on a small square that features a mini statue and pool in the center.

When the weather cooperates, food is served in the garden across from the pool.

We, however, dined inside, where there aren't too many tables. The decoration is fairly plain, and all the staff were dressed in the same black attire. I only learnt afterward that one of these staff members in black was the boss of the establishment – a touch of democratic equality that gave the place extra points in my book. The cover of the menu was made from bamboo, while the placement of the cutlery and glasses on the table was different from the run-of-the-mill pattern. The customer profile, too, was just right, while the service, food and wine was all fantastic. All in all, I was exceptionally pleased by this restaurant, which comes recommended by Michelin, and it quickly became my favorite in Modena.

My starter, Il Nido (The Nest), was, to say the least, magnificent, and the same goes for the tagliatelle with ricotta and spinach (Capelotti al ripeno di stracciatelle con pesto di ricola e creme di rapa rossa).

The entrée, tenerissimo guancialotto di vitello (beef cheek), was certainly not done sous-vide; instead, it really was cooked for hours, which is why it was not only soft but also delicious. The lamb with pecorino cheese and artichoke was also delectable.

Needless to say, the steak in balsamic sauce was also wonderful.

And in keeping with its name, our Terra di Cavignano Superiore Riserva wine was also of superior quality.

If I recall correctly, the menu was solely in Italian, but our black-clad waiter explained in detail all of the choices in English.

"What's your name?" I asked him after the meal.

"Tommy."

"Tommy? That's impossible," I said, engendering surprise.

"Why not?"

"It's not possible because you're a typical Italian."

My persistence prompted him to divulge the truth: His name was Tomasso.

"Now that's more like it," I said, asking what he did there.

Indicating an elegant woman serving dishes at a table, he said: "I'm the boss' husband."

We wished them all the happiness and success in the world...

If you find yourself in Modena, make sure you go to Zelmira!

# The Musician
# Without Listeners

## Locanda Di Sant'Agostino, San Gimignano

The towns that fly the flag for Italy's tourism industry are really charming... Narrow streets... Small squares... Churches... It's as if they bring travelers back to the Middle Ages. Americans devoid of a past especially go crazy for it. You can't deny it, the Italians really know how to market such beauty...

This said, if you've started to lose count of the number of times you've gone, the towns begin to lose their attraction. If you've gone to one, you feel like you've gone to them all. Narrow streets that look the same... Small squares that look the same... Churches that look the same...

One such town is San Gimignano. If you haven't seen it, make sure you do. But if you have, perchance, seen Siena and your time is limited, you could – with apologies to the good people in the Italian tourism industry – give it a pass. The main streets in these towns are now only remarkable for the shops located on them; every brand under the sun now has an outlet in every town! The tourist crowds are now more drawn to the shops, to the point that when you dive into the side streets, there are no crowds. The houses and the balconies there, however, are all the same!

That's why, when my wife is out and about, I tend to wait for her by entering a church and getting a few winks amid the cool silence or sitting down in a café and sipping a sambuca.

With it around noon on this occasion, I opted to wait for her at the Locanda di Sant'Agostino, which is located on a small square that doesn't attract hordes of tourists. The square features a small pool in the middle, but trees and shade are absent. I duly sought respite under an awning in the restaurant's garden and began to sip my sambuca. Across from me, a young man perched on the edge of the pool was playing an accordion. Despite the noontime heat, though, he wasn't even wearing a hat.

"That's his advantage over me," I said to myself: "Youth!"

He played for close to half an hour. The few locals that passed by failed to show their civic pride. They didn't leave any change on the handkerchief he had laid out in front of himself. I finished my drink – how quick a glass can disappear! But who knows how long it seemed for the lad playing under the sun. As I was musing with a bit of a guilty conscience about how time is determined not by hours but by the conditions and psychological atmosphere in which a person finds him or herself, my wife and son arrived.

I related what had happened. My son rose immediately, went over to the musician and – with his Eastern manners and American generosity – left some change before returning. I watched the musician thank him with great warmth before immediately getting up and disappearing.

Years before, I had come across a similar scene. Every morning, a shoe shiner would come and set himself up right across from our home. With his polishing chest beneath a tree, he would shine the shoes of passersby for the whole day. Naturally, he would shine the shoes for everyone in our apartment as well. He would come spontaneously, take our shoes, shine them and bring them back. After years of setting up shop every day right across from us, it was as if he had become one of us – to the degree that if we needed to go somewhere for a few hours, we would leave our son, who was in primary school at the time, in his care. When our son would play with friends in front of the home, the shoe shiner would supervise him. And wouldn't you know that years later, long after we had left that place, he was still there when I came back to visit a friend in the apartment?

I couldn't contain myself; I ran up to him and embraced him. Despite the passage of many years, he asked after my wife and son by name.

I gave him a hefty tip and went into the apartment. I came out half an hour later, only to see that he was gone – just like the young musician in San Gimignano!

It means that he who gets his money disappears from sight...

In the wake of the musician's departure, we ate our meal. Sant'Agostino is a really charming restaurant that makes a really great ribolitta, a Tuscan specialty. In the heat of summer, it's exactly what you need. The two-color vegetable tower was also intriguing. My wife's truffle tagliolini and my truffle risotto were also impeccable. My son also reported enjoying his Rigatoni al ragù di Coniglio. And given that it's Tuscany, one hardly needs to say anything about the wine – all of it is great!

The bill came and we paid it. And then we disappeared from sight...

It means that it's not just he who gets his money that disappears from sight, but also he who gives it!

He without money is lost completely!

# The Town With Streets The Scent Of Citrus

## Kortan, Bodrum

We were in high school at the time, and we'd just come back from summer holiday.

Everyone was telling everyone else about where they'd gone and what they'd done during the summer break.

After everyone had finished telling their story, we turned to our one friend who had been silently taking it all in.

"Where did you go?"

"I didn't go anywhere; I stayed at home!"

"How terrible!"

"There was nothing terrible about it. Our place there…" he began to explain.

Goodness gracious! The classmate who had just been sitting silently in the corner couldn't stop talking about his hometown. The sea there was such that you wanted to drink it! The sand there was such that sunbathers thought they were lying down in a bed made of bird feathers! The streets there were such that the scent of citrus was everywhere!

"Enough already, you can only go so far! Do streets ever smell like citrus? You must really think we're stupid," we said, giving our classmate a good thrashing. These cute little beat-downs were an inseparable part of boarding school…

The place he was talking about was Bodrum.

And what did I see when I went some years later? If anything, our classmate had undersold the place, rather than exaggerate it! Bodrum was a small, little town. When you reached the top of a long, meandering and difficult road, you had the chance to behold the magnificent castle, unparalleled sand and fantastic natural beauty below you. As you descended the hill, you got to dive right into all of this beauty. And our classmate wasn't lying; there really was an incredible scent from the orange, mandarin orange and lemon trees!

The houses were two stories tall and bedecked in white paint. They said no one ever locked their doors at night because there was no such thing as theft. There was just one sizable pension, as most of the small number of visitors were hosted in private homes. I still remember the refreshing coolness of the bedsheets and the scent of mandarin orange cologne next to the sink...

The small population of the town largely subsisted on the sea and diving for sponges. The café on the shore served as a place to gather over tea, both for people preparing to set sail and those returning to land. Nearby, on the narrow roads leading to the café, there were a few shops selling handicrafts and sponges. Still, people were a bit melancholy, and why would they not be? The locals of what outsiders saw as a "charming seaside town" earned their living in difficult maritime conditions. How many people went diving for sponges and never returned – or, even if they did, were never quite the same again? Perhaps this is why they were melancholic, solemn and dignified; they had become acquainted with the blows dealt by life. These blows made every woman and man into philosophers of the coast. They would gather to drink rakı in the evenings in a few meyhanes, as the newly picked peppers, eggplant, herbs and melons would be more than enough for mezes. The star of such evening spreads would be fish that were freshly caught that day – or perhaps just moments before! And if an oud players happened to come your way, you'd reckon you were even a singer as you shouted out all your pent-up emotion.

That was the Bodrum of the 1960s...

After that, Bodrum grew to become one of Europe's most prominent tourism centers.

Despite all this, the Dinç Pension, the largish inn that I saw when I first went there, is still there... So is the Denizciler (Sailors') Café...

The Kortan Meyhane is still there too... Kortan is one of the fish restaurants boasting the best views of Bodrum Castle. While sipping your drink, you'll be enchanted by the beauty of the castle lit up at night.

Its fare is like that of everyone else; it's the same mezes and the same fish. But those not expecting something really exceptional won't have any complaints – we certainly have never had any; the beauty of the surrounding nature has always filled us up first.

One time, my wife went to the ladies' room after our meal. After she washed her hands, we left the restaurant and lost ourselves in the crowds of Bodrum. We had walked a little ways until she suddenly let out a scream:

"Oh no, my ring!"

While washing her hands, she had removed her ring and forgotten it there. We hurried back immediately, but half an hour had passed; someone could have come in after her, taken it and disappeared.

Full of worry, we entered the restaurant, where the boss was on hand, chuckling.

"Forgot your ring, didn't you?"

We were shocked.

"It's something that happens a lot here," he continued. "That's why I go into the washroom every time a lady comes out to see if something's been forgotten!"

We took the ring and thanked him.

When an institution turns such character into a tradition, its life is likely to last long!

The next time I'm back, I'll invite the classmate who first told us about Bodrum and invite him to Kortan if he's still living in the area. After our meal, I won't have the energy anymore to give him a good thrashing, but I could push him into the sea right on the doorstep.

Traditions have to continue, after all, don't they?

# What's "Normale" In Portofino And "Normal" In Adana

## The Stella, Portofino

I love Northern Italy.
It's beautiful...
It's civilized...
Its people are cultured...
The Teatro Alla Scala is located here.

We decided to jet off to Portofino one summer when global warming wasn't yet a topic du jour.
We booked an Istanbul-Milan-Genoa flight with Alitalia, after which we planned to travel to Portofino by land.
That's what we did, but we had a huge suitcase when we boarded in Istanbul and none when we arrived in Genoa.
We made a beeline for the "lost luggage" counter, where they made us fill in a bunch of forms, but they weren't surprised at all. "Normale," they said.

We had arrived in Milan with an Airbus and taken a small plane for our connecting flight.
As we hovered around the lost luggage counter as somber as football supporters whose team had just been dealt a massive defeat, we ran into the pilot of our small plane. As if he would know the magic answer, we asked him about our luggage.
He responded coolly: "Don't worry, normale..."

Bereft of hope, we hopped into a taxi to head to our famous hotel, the Imperiale, in Santa Margerita Ligura. We had but a small bag and the thick clothes we had on when we left Istanbul in the morning. But the weather in Ligura was very hot, and it was abundantly clear that we weren't dressed for the occasion.

We explained our situation at the reception. Dividing her time between signing us in and attempting to console us, the beautiful lady at reception pronounced:

"Don't worry, it'll show up... Normale..."

After enjoying a great meal on the hotel terrace, which overlooked a sea that was bathed in moonlight, we retired to bed.

As soon as we woke up the next day we rushed to the concierge and explained our situation and asked what we could do about our missing luggage. The answer was the same:

"Don't worry, it'll show up... Normale..."

I was beginning to get aggravated.

"Everyone is like 'don't worry, it'll show up... Normale...' We don't have any toothbrushes, shirts and medication! There is nothing 'normale' about this! How and when will this bag get here?

"In a couple of days... Normale..."

To avoid going crazy or developing a rash due to our overly warm attire, we headed straight for the luxurious shops in Portofino to buy clothes (N.B.: There are no cheap stores in Portofino). We bought a couple of T-shirts, shorts and runners ... Though it was only a handful of items, it cost us a couple of days' worth of hotel accommodation!

Still, at a pharmacy, we easily purchased some pills that we couldn't hope to get in America or England without a prescription... Forza Italia!

We spent the day swimming at the beach of the Imperiale, where it's forbidden to move your sunbed even an inch, next to a sea that was being steadily polluted by hundreds of boats that were entering and leaving port.

With mourning futile, we repaired to a well-recommended restaurant in the evening: The Stella. The staff at the hotel said it was frequented by the "jet set."

They say that "waiters, barbers and cab drivers know everything better than anyone else;" I saw this theory in practice at Portofino. As we had done with everyone else who had crossed our path, we related our tale of woe to our waiter. If you are in pain, don't you share it with everyone? Our waiter offered the customary "normale" to begin with, just like all the others, but, thank God, he revealed the trick of the trade. The fact was that they never loaded huge bags onto the small plane while switching planes in Milan, sending them instead by land afterwards. Since this was an ordinary practice that was known to everyone, it was considered "normale."

We were relieved; we had another drink, left a fat tip and headed back to the hotel.

The next morning, we got the news that our luggage had arrived. We were happy. As a bonus, we even got the chance to somewhat renew our wardrobe!

Half a continent away, Adana is a city famous for its kebabs.

We were there on business...We made reservations at a kebab restaurant that was recommended to us. Indeed, the kebabs were really sumptuous.

I hadn't noticed it, but my wife had: There was some kind of commotion at the next table. A women was glancing around with trepidation, occasionally pacing about the restaurant. Her face was ashen!

Afterwards, I asked for the check but the waiter said in a strict manner:

"No. You cannot leave without tasting our baklava."

"But I'm full and about to burst!"

"Don't worry; I'll prepare something so special it will remove that fullness and you'll even want to start eating again."

He said it in such an authoritative manner that I even risked starting the meal again.

"Very well then," I said in desperation.

Our baklava arrived; it was good but we barely ate it. We had swollen up like a balloon. The waiter came holding a glass half-full with lemon juice, filled the rest with mineral water and ordered us to drink it in one go. We did as we were told!

Honest to God, half an hour later, it was as if we hadn't eaten anything. Everything we had eaten had been digested. We felt as light as a feather. We almost started eating again.

But if it wasn't for that unfortunate incident!

The woman with the nervous face at the next table got up and went downstairs.

We heard two gunshots. A woman screamed!

We looked at the waiter with fear. He went about his job as if nothing had happened.

"What happened?" we said.

"They shot the woman! It's normal around here!"

He continued to set out the knives and forks!

The moral of the story is:

Every country...

Every hotel...

Every restaurant...

Can have its own "normal."

The best thing to do is be prepared for surprises.

# On Easily Convinced Husbands And Customers

## Dva Jelena, Belgrade

Stefan Martens translates my articles into English. That's because my English doesn't extend much beyond "How are you? Fine, thank you." When I wrote a blog, they really liked Stefan's translations, but there's something else I like about him – let me explain:

He recently got married, and we passed along our congratulations and well wishes for the future. In all honesty, because he took forever to find a place to live, he was subjected to my pontifications along the lines of "when we were your age, we did it like this and that," but he took this in his stride and didn't make much of a retort due to the difference in age.

But this is how the part about him that I like came to the fore: Whenever I say something, he objects politely. If I insist on something, he then goes for consultations with his wife before returning to me: "Fine, my wife's convinced me, we can go with that." For crying out loud, I've been married for close to 50 years, and I don't remember ever being convinced this easily by my wife – and this guy's just been married for a couple of days! But in the end, it's not a bad thing for spouses to surrender to each other. Stefan showed his smarts, apparently taking refuge in the formula of "surrender and be comfortable." Back in our day though...
I'll leave it up to you as to whether it's a good thing or a bad thing for husbands to be easily convinced by their wives. As I started off on my "back in our day" pontifications, the way they used to persuade customers at restaurants and bars back in the day came to mind... It'd be better if I just related that!

In days gone by, there were nightclubs that were different than those of today; I'm talking about the years when women and men didn't get that close to each other. Villagers from the surrounding towns generally came to these types of bars in the big cities. Naturally, there was a greater abundance of patrons hailing from the villages when they got a hold of some money come harvest time. Those coming to these clubs sometimes came to eat but more often than not, they came for entertainment after a meal. The entertainment typically took this form: After the patron sat down at the table, he would choose one of the hostesses in the vicinity and invite her to the table. The woman would drink a lot of lower-percentage alcohol while correspondingly getting her customer to imbibe stronger alcohol – all while inflating the tab. They would while away the time chatting, and there were a few who would accompany the resident orchestra's poorly played music with dance. That was it!

Now, "that was it" could be perceived as condescending, but it's not far off the mark. Is it far off the mark for such people given that the conversation the men engaged in was not of the type they could do with their wives in the village, that there was dancing and, if they weren't married, that this was one of the few chances for them to inhale the scent of a woman? Of course, the bill didn't come cheap; some of them accepted the bottom line, while some of them contested the matter.

Young single men generally had just a couple beer during the course of the event, but that didn't save them from what came next.
"What the hell is this?"
"The bill, sir."
"You think I'm blind? I can see that it's the bill. How do you get a bill like that from two beer?"
The waiter would explain the matter, noting the music, the woman, the nuts, the flowers on the table…
"Really? Did I tell you to put flowers on the table?"
"You did not, but you did not ask that they be removed!"

At this juncture, if the customer was persuaded to pay the bill without dragging out proceedings further, so much the better for everyone. If he opted not to pay the bill, then it came time to "persuade" him. Efforts to persuade the customer that there had not been a miscalculation with the bill generally ended with a broken nose and a black eye for the patron, as well as a trip to the local constabulary.

Because I witnessed such methods of persuasion when I was young, I tend to get uneasy if I'm the recipient of more attention than usual at a bar or restaurant, or if flowers or mezes that I haven't ordered come to the table, or if musicians congregate at my side for longer than necessary.

That's exactly what happened at Dva Jelena.

It wasn't as if I wasn't entertaining concerns as I inspected the menu at this cute restaurant in Belgrade's Skardalija quarter. There were names of food in a language I don't know and prices in a currency that I'm not familiar with… Because of that – and as far I understood – I asked for simple dishes. The waiter, however, objected, recommending different choices, increasing my level of worry.
"This guy's going to give us the tourist price," I told myself. Soon, though, I accepted my fate and accepted his recommendations.
Soon after, a massive earthenware casserole bowl appeared with an amount of meat and vegetables in it that we could only hope to consume over a week at home. Of course, the dish's appearance served to strengthen my premonitions about the nature of the bill to come. And, as luck would have it, wouldn't the Gypsy orchestra start to play at our table right out of the blue?

For as long as I can remember, I've always loved the Gypsy air of the Balkans. I couldn't resist and gave them a tip a bit on the early side. But wouldn't you know that that just got them more excited. They probably thought the money was really meaningful, as they went as far as playing our national anthem. I mean, really, you rise and stand when the national anthem is played, but were we supposed to stand at attention when all the other tables were laughing and dancing amid the abundant food and drink? Anyway, we managed to settle the matter, sending the orchestra on its way.

By the end of the night, it was time to learn what the damage was: The bill came, I looked at it, tried to figure it out, looked at it again and called the waiter over to explain the matter. The bill for our feast might not have been even half of what it would have been in other places. If I find myself in Belgrade again and you need to get a hold of me, come find me at the Dva Jelena...

> "What the hell is this?"
> "The bill sir".
> "You think I'm blind? I can see that it's the bill. How do you get a bill like that from two beer?"

# Conchiglia The Destination, Il Postino The Consolation

## Il Postino, Procida Island

The Conchiglia was a restaurant on Procida that had come with recommendations.
An island in the Bay of Naples, Procida is a small speck of land right next to Ischia. With buildings falling apart and even its pastel colors fading, the closest place that it would resemble would be a Sicilian town. But it's precisely these characteristics that steal the show, drawing tourists all and sundry. Films are made here, and it's as if everything is a theater prop.

I made reservations at the Conchiglia for 7.30 in the evening. I got someone to call one more time from the hotel before we headed out.
"Tonight we're opening at 8!" they exclaimed.
Not to worry – we would find something to amuse ourselves with around there. The only issue is that the restaurant is some distance away from the Procida harbor, meaning reaching it is no easy task.
"Tell them not to worry – we'll send a boat to pick them up," the restaurant informed the hotel employee that called on our behalf. "But we won't pick them up from the ferry dock but a fisherman's cove. Make sure they're there at 8."

That sounded good to me. We boarded the 5 p.m. ferry from Ischia, arriving on Procida half an hour later. We moseyed about the harbor and its environs before heading to the designated fishermen's cove to wait for the boat. But wait as we might, there was nothing doing. Worried that we'd come to the wrong spot, I queried one of the fishermen there.

"No, you're in the right place," he reassured us. "Conchiglia's boat is orange and it'll pull up to the men you see talking over there in front of the Ristorante Il Postino." As it was, the fishermen's cove was really small, and we could comfortably survey all the boat traffic from our location. It would be impossible to miss the boat. I called our hotel in Ischia once more to find out what was going on.

After speaking with the restaurant, they informed us that the boat would be there in 20 minutes. Even so, the timing would entail inhaling our food to avoid missing the last ferry back.

Alas, we were denied even that pleasure. No one came to pick us up or even provide news. Abandoning our hopes for the Conchiglia, we elected to grab a quick bite to eat at one of the fish restaurants close by. Duly, we selected the one right in front of where we had been waiting: Ristorante Il Postino.

I knew that the film Il Postino: The Postman had been filmed on Procida. The restaurant appeared to have attempted to capitalize on the name of the emotional film by director Michael Radford about famous poet Pablo Neruda (Philippe Noiret), his postman, Mario (Massimo Troisi), and the latter's lover, Beatrice (Maria Grazia Cucinotta), but it's not something that I paid much attention to at first. But after eating out on the pier, what did I find when I went inside to use the facilities? Nothing but the postman's bag front and center – as well as many pictures from the film. After all, wasn't this the place where Mario's love, Beatrice, worked? Wasn't this the place where the film's most emotional scenes were filmed? Standing there, the whole film flashed before my eyes once more. It was as if we saw ourselves looking on at the next table as Mario was trying to share his feelings to Beatrice.

The standing of the restaurant suddenly rose in our estimation... In truth, we had given the fried sardines and grilled skewered calamari a high grade, but after pondering the fact that we had consumed this on the set of a wonderful film, we raised the grade even higher. Soon, there was nary a memory of Conchiglia's disrespect. On the contrary, we were more than happy that they hadn't come to pick us up – after all, there's a silver lining to everything.

As we were perusing the photographs from the film adorning the walls, jogging our memory of the movie in the process, we suddenly realized that we were going to be late for the ferry. We made it back to the harbor as quick as our legs would carry us – only to find the ticket booth closed. "We're hooped now," we lamented. Apart from the prospect of the money spent on our comfortable room in Ischia going to waste, I hadn't even noticed a hotel decent enough to spend the night on Procida.

We looked right and left and spied a young couple engaged in a passionate embrace on a bench. Reluctantly, I distracted them momentarily from their amorous affections. I explained the situation, and inquired as to our possible course of action. The lad, a not particularly bright one, could only offer, "Really, I have no clue." The girl he was embracing was quieter (although I wouldn't have expected her to have been particularly excited about much of anything given the overall quality of the guy).
"Don't worry," she said. "There's a tobacconist a 100 meters up. They sell ferry tickets; you can get one there."
"Are you sure?"
"Of course I am, I'm from here!" she announced triumphantly.
The only thing I didn't do was kiss the girl. We set off at once for the place she indicated. Because I was a 100-meter runner in high school, I'm well acquainted with the distance. To tell you the truth, I had no success of note, but at least I know how far 100 meters are! Scanning to the right, we saw that there was no tobacconist; scanning to the left, we saw that there was no tobacconist... We walked a bit further, and I realized the woman had certainly not measured the road in meters! After proceeding about 200 meters, I started to harbor doubts. I inquired in a shop about the tobacconist.
"It's just a bit ahead to the right," came the reply.

At least we were on the right path! We continued at pace, but despite keeping an eagle eye out, there was neither a tobacconist's nor a liquor shop. After putting about 500 meters between ourselves and the pier, we asked another shopkeeper. An elderly man took pity on our plight and said, "Come, I'll show you." Leading us, he showed us the promised shop.

We entered, all in a fluster.

"Two tickets to Ischia, please!"

The man shot me a glare. After indicating his shop's sign, he pronounced: "We sell cigarettes, not ferry tickets."

"But they told us you did!" we cried.

"Who did?"

"A girl."

"Which girl?"

"A girl that was making out!"

"Mamma mia... Do they already know this much about making out?"

Anyways, the fatherly figure reassured us: "Don't worry." He held out a cigarette, offering a couple of drags to ease our worries.

"No thanks, we don't smoke," we said.

He shot a condescending glance that suggested "What on earth are you doing in a tobacconist's if you don't smoke?" but then said the magic words.

"The ticket booth will open soon. They're kind of slackers, but go back and you'll see."

I considered hugging and kissing the man, but with no time remaining, we ran back the 500 meters and, lo and behold, the ticket booth really had opened. There were just a few minutes until the sailing, but we secured our tickets and boarded as the last passengers!

We finally relaxed when we got onto the deck and felt the breeze from the Bay of Naples on our faces.

I certainly wouldn't have been able to turn down a smoke if someone had offered it though...

# The Atelier Robuchon And The Michelin Criteria

## Atelier Robuchon, Paris

The Oscars for the world of gastronomy are Michelin's macaroons.

It was at the beginning of the 20th century when tire manufacturer Michelin started promoting road-side restaurants to increase sales of its products. This intelligent tire marketing idea soon found its way into the world of gastronomy. In 1931, restaurants began receiving a promotional boost with a grading system. At first, it was just restaurants in Western Europe that were awarded stars, but the system soon spread to encompass America, Japan and China.

These days, the system works like this:

Inspectors that all join Michelin after succeeding on a variety of tests move from restaurant to restaurant – sometimes on their own and sometimes together – appraising the premises' adherence to the principles determined by Michelin before duly filing a report. Their identities are secret. Sometimes, however, after conducting their audit and settling their bill, they out themselves by asking to see the kitchen or clarifying some issues in discussion with the chef. On average, an inspector covers 30,000 kilometers, spends 160 nights in a hotel and dines in 250 restaurants every year. In 2015, 8,400 restaurants were inspected in France in this fashion alone. It's a massive number and a serious business.
Restaurants that are deemed worthy of a grade are awarded one, two or three stars. The meaning of these stars – known as macaroons – is as follows:

One star: A very good restaurant for its class that's worth stopping on the road for a bite to eat.

Two stars: The perfect restaurant that's worth changing directions just to dine there.
Three stars: An extraordinary restaurant that's worth just setting out on the road for.
The grading is conducted according to this criteria:
1. Quality of the product on offer,
2. Quality of the cooking and taste,
3. Reflection of the chef's uniqueness in the dish,
4. Balance between price and quality,
5. Quality of service

But it all boils down to this: The taste of the meal!

When choosing a restaurant, "the taste of the meal" is naturally a must, but I'm not sure if it's sufficient. Should the Michelin observation grades, which originated in the first half of the 1900s, remain restricted to such a narrow field of vision, or should they be expanded to respond to the changing needs and various expectations of today?
Personally, I take a broader range of factors into consideration when making a choice. I start off the matter with the ease of making a reservation; at some restaurants, you can only make a reservation by phone. But for someone coming from outside of Europe to Paris, making a restaurant reservation by phone is hardly the easiest task. At the same time, the jury is still out on whether new developments such as coupons have facilitated matters for customers or just become a means to extra earnings for those that created the system. Likewise, I look to see whether a restaurant's accessibility, valet parking, waiting time at the door, coat-check services and profile of the clientele match with what's expected, along with other factors such as the waiter's demeanor post-tip.

Naturally, there's also the issue of who has the ability to sample the "taste of the meal!"
For instance, does a person in a wheelchair who enjoys wining and dining and has the financial means to frequent expensive restaurants have the opportunity to enter the restaurant, or is the right to sample its renowned delights only the preserve of the able-bodied?
Atelier Joel Robuchon is a Paris restaurant with two Michelin stars.

For gastronomes tired of the classic French bistro, it's a small and chic restaurant sporting a warm and modern internal design that is largely red and black. The establishment consists of just a bar and eight to 10 tables. Locals generally sit at the bar, where the food is cooked right in front of you. It's quite wonderful. Foreign visitors, meanwhile, generally sit at the tables. It's bursting a bit at the gills, but so are most bistros... Without question, the checkmarks in favor of the restaurant are not restricted to simply its warm, friendly and modern interior! Remember, the thing that actually wins macaroons is the "taste of the meal." My dish was fantastic, both in terms of taste and presentation – if it hadn't been, the restaurant certainly wouldn't have warranted two macaroons.

As such, there's no need to dwell too much on the food. But that's not to say there aren't shortcomings hindering it from reaching three stars or threatening to reduce it to a single star. When you're in a rarified air, people will involuntarily search for deficiencies. Accordingly, I'd like to note a few nuances, since it's only possible to differentiate between the "very good" and the "perfect" by observing the nuances.
At this restaurant in France, a country that is one of the spiritual guardians of bread, three types of bread came to the table, but all three were run of the mill and, moreover, none of them were brown!
The green salad was far saltier than necessary, although it's possible to see this as a choice, rather than a shortcoming, on the part of the chef given that it's salt and butter that give French cuisine an extra dash of taste.

But the porcelain decanter with the sauce for the meat was so hot it was impossible to hold, meaning there was no choice but to eat a third of the meal without sauce!

The mashed potatoes, which had the consistency of refined cream, were brought in a small, four-sided serving dish. Because there was no spoon, however, it was necessary to extract the liquid garniture with a fork, which is no easy task considering the serving dish in question.

At the table next to us were two perfect English gentlemen of about 75 to 80 years of age. They ate with elegance and engaged in discussion with enjoyment. All of a sudden, the handle of the wine glass of the man next to me broke; the waiter ran immediately and poured the wine into another glass. What he should have done was take the broken glass and bring more wine in a new glass. It's not as if I wasn't curious about the brand of glass the 80-year-old was drinking from, but I chose not to embarrass the establishment by asking. I merely proffered to my red-faced neighbor, "What strength you have, sir." The response was immediate:

"Ooo, given that I've broken the first glass, who knows what I would do if I had a lot more!"

The misfortune to befall the restaurant on the wine front was not restricted to this, however, as what happened at the table soon infected its 70-something neighbor – that is, me. I had ordered a glass of the 2011 Château Neuf Du Pape. The wine that came didn't satisfy me particularly, but I remained silent. When I asked for the bill, though, I asked to see the bottle of wine in question. They brought it – but it was an unopened bottle! In the best-case scenario, they had probably brought me the remnants of the last previous bottle, as the wine had oxidized somewhat. I mentioned this politely, at which point they forthwith exclaimed that they would replace the bottle.

"I didn't come to drink wine for free, I came to drink the wine I desired... Thank you, but I don't want it," I said, rejecting the offer. Of course, the bill that arrived featured a wine "on the house!"

I don't know if Michelin's inspectors pay attention to these sorts of nuances, or do they just mainly look at the "taste of the meal?"

I don't know, is there any equality in terms of benefiting from the "taste of the meal" in France? For example, does someone in a wheelchair have the right to come and partake in the abundance that others are able to enjoy? Are nuances like these taken into consideration?

Despite having a street-level entry, the fact that Atelier Robuchon is a small restaurant means it's probably impossible for them to provide room for someone in a wheelchair. While we were thinking this, we saw a cute dog that had sat beneath one of the bar stools, most likely sharing in his master's enjoyment.

We left with this impression of the restaurant, which offers ease to wealthy and healthy people, as well as lucky dogs...

# What Kind Of Man Would You Like?

## Le Balcon, Paris

There's a song by Lynda Lemay: I'm looking for a man of 50!

The song expresses the desires – or more than that, the rebellion and cry – of a woman who is fed up with the ineptitude and immaturity of young men, as well as their failure to appreciate a woman's value and how they just generally wear a woman down.

She says – well, actually, she says and wants a lot, but let me summarize it for her – this:
"I'm looking for a man of 50... Someone who's seen everything, who's had dreams that have been broken and abandoned... Someone who knows what he wants and what he could find in return... Someone who's wined and dined, been with plenty of naked women, and been satisfied so that he's not looking for much more... Someone who knows the time remaining him is shorter than what has passed already... Someone who's now free of making up lies for the sake of foolish feelings... Someone who doesn't take himself too seriously... Someone who will truly and quietly be able to love me... Someone who's made the odd misstep but not a person who's done things behind someone else's back... He doesn't have to be perfect, but I'm looking for a 50-year-old man to be my own."

I have to admit as a man that the youthful versions of ourselves caused a lot of trouble for women. Immaturity... A lack of consideration in trying to get someone to accept you... The pettiness that stems from the struggles of life... You can't even count them all! For this reason, it's no surprise that women, who mature much sooner than men, feel a need to look for men who will protect, embrace and take care of them in compassion instead of searching for contemporaries that are only likely to exhaust and wear them down.

This is one side of the coin!

But now to the other side of the coin: It is not uncommon to encounter an andropausal man going on 50 who is waiting for such a woman – only to feel aggrieved and bemoan his fate when she doesn't appear, all while feeling a need for another glass as he contemplates the matter and grows pettier, harder and ruder. What's more, is it so rare for a mature man to abandon his settled life when a young woman, whom he assumes has been searching for him, emerges before him, only for him to seek to return amid regrets – sometimes succeeding but more oftentimes not?

In the end, who does this tumult affect the most? Aren't women the ones usually left having to pick up the pieces? I wonder, is a young madame singer aware of these realities when searching for a mature 50-year-old? If she is, would she still continue her quest?
I'm relating all of this for this reason:
Would there be such a thing as songs if these desires, ebbs and flows, loves, sorrows, expectations and disappointments did not exist?
If there were no songs, would halls be constructed for their performance?

The Philharmonie de Paris is one place in which such songs are performed, embracing both classical musical concerts and other genres. It opened in January 2015, showcasing an ultra-modern appearance. In its own estimation, it neither resembles a shoebox like Vienna's Musikverein, or a bunch of grapes like the Berlin Philharmonic. Thank goodness the Austrians and the Germans don't turn to the French and say, "But your trains don't run on time… More than that, they're not clean either," when they hear this. Well, they probably say it, but I just haven't heard.

In the complex, which is available for all types of cultural activities, there are three places for food and drink: Le Balcon, Les Gourmandise de l'Atelier and Le Café des Concerts.

Le Balcon is the one that stands out. Located on the floor beneath the newly constructed concert hall, it has a view out onto the greenery but evening concert-goers naturally can't see anything but the lights. The most notable thing about the restaurant is its chairs, which are decorated with pastel-colored pieces of ragged fabric that have been brought together. It's as if you're sitting on a tree leaf. The fare on offer has been selected to be consumed quickly. Some opt for a plate of mixed cold cuts and others for a salad. Few, however, head to the hall without first completing their wine.

We chose to go with the flow as well, ordering a plate with cheese and meat, as well as a mixed salad. The meat was a bit rough and hard but was made passible with the help of a 2014 Sancerre Domaine Vacheron. The service was also exceptionally fast and delivered with a smile. The affair sends everyone into a cheerful and comfortable mood before heading to the big hall for the performance.

Ushers, meanwhile, check your ticket in front of the elevator, facilitating matters. The only thing that irked me was the section entering the main hall. I reckon they thought they would go for the minimalist look, only to either get a bit too carried away or fail to follow in the footsteps of Japanese minimalist masters, as the straight-as-an-arrow, pure white walls and doors make you feel as if you're entering a factory storage unit rather than a concert hall.

But you soon forget everything when you enter and abandon yourself to the flow of the music.
Or perhaps you're busy making calculations about age and life… Who knows?

# Luna Caprese At Le Grotelle

## Le Grotelle, Capri

Umberto Square is known as the "Piazzetta" for short by Capri locals.

It's a small square that is full of cafés. They weren't as ubiquitous before, but on my last visit, you could hardly turn around without bumping into tables or chairs. Even if the municipal hall looking out onto the square weren't on the second floor, it would be impossible to gain entry for all the tables and chairs, but – between you and me – maybe that might just be for the better.

A number of narrow streets radiate out to the right and the left from the Piazzetta, although it would be generous to actually term any of these as "streets." On one, after a narrow entry, you're immediately confronted by stairs; after negotiating them, you turn to the right and find yourself on a "streetling." I say a "streetling" because it's so narrow that if two couples coming from opposite directions while walking arm in arm (because it is Capri, after all) ran into each other, one of the pairs would need to bend over to the let the other pass. As you can guess, in terms of motor vehicles, only a motorcycle at most can frequent such areas. Despite this narrowness, there are still shops on both sides of the streetling. After a while, these shops give way to houses with gardens. The whole way from the Piazzetta, you first ascend the stairs before continuing on your way up a steep hill.

You walk on and on... You walk on and on without respite; if you're used to walking, you'll go at least half an hour. If you don't frequent your local gym or you're not particularly enamored with walking, this duration will increase in accordance with your age and weight.

But you know where you're going: Le Grotelle, a small, family-run restaurant. That's all well and good, but who in their mind would have the bright idea of opening a restaurant in a place so far away that's not accessible by car? Who would traipse this far along just for some grub?

After dragging yourself huffing and puffing up the hill, you finally come to an open-air restaurant on the edge of town: an impossibly cute "guinguette" inside a forest that is close to the Arco Naturale. Bougainvillea surrounds the tables at the restaurant, located on one of Capri's highest hills. Looking down from the craggy rocks is not for the faint of heart. Before you lies the deep-blue Mediterranean extending all the way to the Sorrento coast – a view that is impossible to resist. Shortly after beholding this beauty, the light will fade; if you're lucky (and we were), there in front of you might be a crimson full moon of the type known as a "Luna Rosso" in song. Words fail such beauty. All you want is for the wine to come immediately, and even looking through the wine list is a distraction from the sight before you.

"A bottle of white from the Campania region, please."

A Faranghina comes. Produced on the island, it's been cooled to just the right temperature. As you take your first sips, you feel a wave of relief wash over you; nothing remains of the fatigue from the journey or, indeed, of anything else. Toward 9.30, the restaurant is completely full. Soon, you're embarrassed that you ever deigned to think of "who in their mind would have the bright idea of opening a restaurant in a place so far away that's not accessible by car." Those coming to assume their places at the table first salute the chef standing at attention next to the wood-fire oven, addressing him by name, or, in some cases, embracing him. After that, they return to their own private worlds, full of laughter, mirth and boisterous conversation. Soon, you're also enveloped in this atmosphere, joining the conversation with those at the tables to your right and left.

We enjoyed some really great food here. And after having an "orata" (gilt-head bream) cooked in the wood-fire oven, we understood why everyone else was embracing and saluting the chef.

The only thing missing on this night of the full moon was someone to sing Neapolitan songs accompanied by a mandolin. When the owner came to our table, I noted this oversight, humming the part from Peppino di Capri's famous song about the full moon that goes "o luna... Luna Caprese." Not one to sit on the sidelines, the owner also joined in, picking up and carrying on the tune. And as if on cue, wouldn't the other tables all join in, too? Raising a collective glass to the full moon in Capri, the whole garden sang Luna Caprese (The Full Moon) in unison.

Everything was truly wonderful...

The way there had taken so much out of us... We ascended the stairs and then outlasted the hill, but everything was worth it for this magnificence.

In the end, beauty is certainly not something that's easy to attain.

As he was sending us off, the owner whispered in my ear:

"Signore, what would you like to sing tomorrow night?"

I whispered in his ear in return:

"Look at me," I said. "Forget about singing solo, they even kicked me and my crow-like voice out of the school choir. If I start singing, how much are you willing to pay to keep my mouth shut?"

# A Little Pair Of Socks

## Cafe Arlequin, San Francisco

I generally sleep well. I hit the hay early, sleep an uninterrupted nine hours and get up early.
Whether it's summer or winter, I don't put on pajamas, preferring to wear a thin T-Shirt to bed instead.
But after climbing into bed the other night, I realized how cold I was, even though there was both a blanket and a quilt on top of me, while the heat was also on.

I got up, put on the pajama top and went back to bed, but I just couldn't warm up!
This time, I put on the pajama bottoms and tried to go back to sleep, but that provided no respite either.
"What is this? Am I getting sick?" I thought, putting on my socks as a last resort.
I fell asleep a short time later. The socks had done the trick, sending me off into the realm of sweet dreams...

The requisite warmth that could not be provided by the heater, quilt, blanket and pajamas was provided solely by a small pair of socks!
Sometimes, the things that we dismiss due to their small stature turn out to be far more useful than the things we accord greater importance to due to their greater size. It seems these more minute items turn out to provide more comfort and confidence.

Naturally, it's a similar story with restaurants. Sometimes you see a small and inconspicuous restaurant that you don't take particularly seriously. After having food there, however, your whole viewpoint changes, as it vastly exceeds your initial expectations.
Arlequin is one such restaurant.
Located in San Francisco, it's a place whose exterior is unlikely to set the pulse racing, and you might find

yourself hesitating about whether to even enter. But after going through the door – and if you are fortunate enough to score a table in the garden – you can be sure you're in for a treat. The garden is ever-so-slightly "negligé," retaining its natural look. There are no more than five or six tables in total, all of which are placed some distance from each other. While it would have been possible to insert several more tables into the garden and increase the profits, the owners of Arlequin didn't deign to stoop to such a level – even when there's a queue to find a table! This respect for nature and customers is unlikely to escape your attention, and it will most certainly foster a reciprocal respect on your part. It's a place that offers a chance to sink your teeth into your delectable food and enthusiastically imbibe your wine or beer under a nice autumn sun. What else could a person want?

Arlequin is small and modest. But Arlequin is a restaurant that will deliver much more than you expect. Just like my little socks!

# Harry's Bar Still Capitalizing On La Dolce Vita

## Harry's Bar, Rome

Fellini's La Dolce Vita astounded people in 1960.

The movie revolved around the lives of members of high society in Rome – or carefree, degenerate and rich individuals who described themselves as high society – through the eyes of Marcello Mastroianni, the forefather of the paparazzi.

A wily fox like Fellini steals the hearts of women with a stud like Mastroianni, but would he forget the guys? For them, he introduced a northern bombshell in the shape of Anita Ekberg and "a different kind of beauty" by the name of Anouk Aimée.

The film, which depicted events in Rome's high society that could be categorized as a huge breakdown in morality, was a big hit during its time.

Another movie that resembles this one and reflected the lavish lifestyle in Rome was La Grande Belleza, which I think was made in 2015 – at least that's when I saw it. This Sorrentino movie, which featured the decidedly unhandsome but masterful actor Toni Servillo, was also very successful.

But let me return to La Dolce Vita by way of a book that also touches on this characteristic of Rome, You Are My Life (Sei La Mia Vita), by famous director Ferzan Özpetek. The book, which presents snippets from Rome's gay scene, is even regarded with respect by those who are oblivious to that world, since it was authored by Özpetek, a master storyteller.

One of the main locations in Fellini's La Dolce Vita is the hugely popular Via Veneto.
Harry's Bar is located at the top of this street.

Back in the day, it was a very popular meeting place, and many celebrities were sighted at the venue. Even Frank Sinatra played the piano there.

No doubt Harry's Bar earned itself a pride of place in La Dolce Vita thanks to these qualities. This was the restaurant-bar where night owls came to meet.

When we sat down at Harry's Bar for dinner, it was more than half a century after the movie hit the screens. Via Veneto was not as bright as it once was. Times had changed...Inevitably, the status of Harry's Bar had also changed; it was no longer hosting high society but tourists like us.

However, the restaurant still capitalizes on La Dolce Vita ever so brilliantly! Everywhere you looked, you were faced with a picture from the movie or a memory.

There was a screen across from our table that constantly played scenes from La Dolce Vita and other Italian films or shots of other Italian actors. We recognized all the movies and actors, reciting them as though we were contestants on a game show.

We struck up a conversation with a couple sitting next to us under the screen. They asked us where we were from but admitted to being surprised by the answer. We launched into a hearty conversation. Then they asked us how we recognized so many movies. "Oh, what we don't know!" we uttered, showing off. The guy turned out to be Irish...His wife, Italian – but, strangely, not a very communicative one. Soon the mystery would be revealed.

While we talked and sipped our wine, identifying scenes from the movies and their actors had indeed turned into a national game show. An Italian actor popped onto the screen. We stayed silent because it was a gimme. To our dismay, our neighbors were quiet!

"Go ahead," I said.

"We have no clue!"

When I said, "Well now, sir; fine, you're Irish, so you're off the hook, but madam, how can you not recognize who this is! This is a very famous Italian actor; what kind of an Italian are you? You don't even talk that much." Her husband piped up:

"My wife came to Ireland at a very young age and knows Irish culture better than her own!"

"Well, that explains it," I said and ended the competition right then and there.

As for the food we ate at Harry's Bar... What's the point of food among all these memories?

Still, I would recommend the risotto with champagne...

# The Shares In
# The Elevator

## Stone Tavern, New York

As the guest of an American bank, I had the opportunity to watch the last session of the 20th century at the New York Stock Exchange and the first session of the 21st. Just being able to enter the trading room floor of the world's biggest exchange was unforgettable, but experiencing this exceptional adventure twice – as one century ended and another began – was even more so.

But there's another memory of the stock exchange from my youth that I cannot forget. Back in those days, there were, of course, no digital records in the world of finance. Instead, shares were printed in the hundreds, thousands and hundreds of thousands before being transferred from place to place by truck. Moreover, most of these shares were "to the bearer" – meaning that, like banknotes, they became the property of whoever happened to get their hands on them. As you can guess, protecting the shares was a chore fraught with risk.

One time, my investment bank (I was one of the managers) needed to send a not-so-insignificant number of shares somewhere else. Boxes were prepared for the occasion, and an armored vehicle big enough to transport all these boxes soon appeared downstairs at the entrance, ready for the shares. My two assistants opened the door to the elevator and began loading it with the boxes full of shares issued "to the bearer."

But then, just as they were about to board the elevator themselves after doing all the heavy work of loading in the boxes, the door closed and the lift began to descend: Someone had called for the elevator on the ground floor. Can you imagine the stakes? The bank is located in a place that is full of financial companies; most of those working in the vicinity were only too familiar with the meaning of a "bearer share." So what would happen if some ne'er-do-well down below opened the door, saw the boxes and made off with a bunch?

This is what would happen: They would probably become a millionaire, and we would slave away the rest of our days trying to pay off an unpayable debt!

I still can't fathom how we managed to fly down the stairs in pursuit of the elevator. Still, the building was just three stories, and as the elevator reached the ground floor, we did too. Just as those waiting were about to open the elevator door, we jumped in and formed a cordon in front of the boxes.

What would have happened if it had been a 20-story building in a financial center like Manhattan? In the vicinity of the NYSE, there are – funnily enough – quite a few narrow streets heading to the world's biggest securities exchange and that jungle of skyscrapers that is Manhattan.

On these narrow roads, there are a few low-rise office buildings that feature restaurants interspersed among them. Financial companies tend to host customers for lunch at these eateries, one of which is the Stone Tavern. It's a stomping ground for yuppies of both sexes, and energy and dynamism accordingly reign supreme inside. Sporting décolleté, the waitresses were as beautiful as those at Paris' L'Avenue. Their food, meanwhile, was generally of the variety that could be consumed quickly – I, for one, enjoyed their steak.

But if you asked me what I liked the most, I'd have to say the low-rise buildings in the area. All records might be digital these days, and printed shares and physical deliveries might have gone the way of the dodo... But you can never be too sure: Speaking from experience, I'm one who prefers buildings with few floors in financial areas!

You could call this nostalgia, if you like... I certainly wouldn't object!

> " I had the opportunity to watch the last session of the 20th century at the NYSE and the first session of the 21st. Just being able to enter the trading room floor of the world's biggest exchange was unforgettable, but there's another memory of the stock exchange from my youth that I cannot forget. "

# Eggplant Growers Aren't Paying My Salary!

## Fiorello, New York

During my long working life, I've gotten the opportunity to meet a lot of people and observe a lot of "personalities."

If you asked me to categorize them, it wouldn't be easy; I can only make a few generalizations – there's a type of person that exhibits "boss behavior" and another who is marked by his or her "behavior toward the boss."

Perhaps thanks to the success they have enjoyed in their jobs, some bosses might think that they are – or could be – superior or successful in every situation. These people talk about how much they value the professionals around them, but what they actually value in the latter is the ability to sing the praises of their superiors. What do such bosses want? They want those around them to parrot back their views and to avoid presenting different views or – perish the thought – opinions that contrast with their own. From time to time, they also enjoy playing with those around them and forcing them to jump through hoops. Among professionals, they are some who facilitate such behavior and some who don't.

One time, I overheard a young boss speaking at the next table over. That day, the boss was all smiles, and it was clear that he wanted to have some fun at others' expense and enjoy the trappings of his "superiority." He noted that he really enjoyed eggplant, prompting a lightning-quick response from one of the senior managers at the table:
"Yes, sir. You can make more than 20 different dishes from eggplant, and they're all as great as the next."
Getting into his stride, the boss said: "I like moussaka the most, but not the Greek way with béchamel sauce

– that's too rich."

"It's true, sir, moussaka is one of the world's most delicious meals, so long as it's not too rich!" his yes-man quickly answered. "Béchamel sauce doesn't suit moussaka at all!"

"There are benefits to eggplant..." the boss threw out.

"But of course, sir! It's low in calories, and because it's high in fiber, it's good for digestion. What's more, it also has vitamins A, B and C."

"That's not to say that there aren't drawbacks," the boss said, sharply steering the conversation in the opposite direction.

"Of course, sir, there are drawbacks indeed," his manager said, rushing to do his own 180. "Because it contains nicotine, it's like smoking a cigarette when you eat it. And frying it raises the cholesterol, and if oil escapes from the pan while it's frying, it could even start a fire!"

"It's best to just not eat it at all!" the boss concluded.

"You're quite right there, sir," the manager said, tripping over himself in his obsequiousness. "Let's tell our cook to make less eggplant-based dishes from now on!"

Following the meal, I got a chance to have a word with the senior manager.

"Really, whatever your boss said, you just parroted it back to him," I said. "He says, 'I like it,' and you say, 'I like it.' Then he goes the other way and says, 'I don't like it,' and you do a U-turn too. He played you, pure and simple. How could you let him do this?"

"Look," he started. "Eggplant growers aren't paying my salary, my boss is. If he says black is white, then I do too. It's that simple."

I felt sorry for him because I know, from my experience, that it's possible to be successful without farming your personality out to someone else.

We were downing a quick meal at Fiorello, since a glass of wine along with some vegetables seemed like a great idea before heading to a concert. I especially liked the Sicilian eggplant caponata – to the extent that I recalled the story above while eating it. Mind you, I can't quite remember whether we were going to see Placido Domingo or Cecilia Bartoli that night.

Café Fiorello is a charming restaurant/bar across from the Lincoln Center. The café draws quality customers, most of whom come to watch performances at the center. Diners either down something quickly before heading to the concert, ballet or opera, or come afterwards to have a drink in more comfortable surroundings and continue the vibe from the performance. And for those dining before the show, waiters always bring the bill along with the food, lest customers be late.

Fiorello mostly serves Italian dishes and snacks, with my favorite being their pizzas; they're as thin as can be and supremely tasty.

Unless you've been to a performance at the Lincoln, I wouldn't say that you've been to New York. And if you haven't done so yet, I suggest you arrange an evening there. Whether before or after a show, head to Fiorello, sit down and top off your evening with some food and drink and the performance. And if you have something with eggplant, remember what I said.

It's not worth farming yourself out to someone else for the sake of an extra morsel of food, just like it's not worth crushing the personality of someone else just to gain an extra inch on them!

After all, can you take any of it with you?

# Woman Chefs' "Soft Spot" For Children

## La Dame De Pic, Paris

A friend of mine, a certain Monsieur Milard, lives a true bourgeois existence.

He knows and likes to live well.

He has a seat in row two, right in front of the orchestra, at Opera Garnier, so he's someone who really knows his art and literature. He opened his home to a fine arts student named Alphonse and says he's quite happy to cook him food and wait on him.

There's no restaurant in Paris that he doesn't know.

And just like me, he takes Ricard as an apéro. One day, when we were having a chat while sipping our Ricards at La Colombe, he asked me, "Do you like La Dame de Pic?"

"Are you kidding, Milard?" I responded. "Is it possible to not like Pushkin? What's more, it's a story that resonates just as much today. The guy wrote about the consequences of greed a century and a half ago, but it's as if he just wrote it yesterday. It's as if he was talking about today's overambitious people. The Pikoyeva Dama is the only thing I haven't seen – may Tchaikovsky forgive me."

"What on earth are you talking about?"

"I'm answering your question, Milard. Are you not listening to me, or do not understand my French?"

When peals of laughter ensued, I finally understood: He wasn't talking about Pushkin's famous short story

La Dame de pique, he was talking about the famous restaurant in Paris, "La Dame de Pic!"

I duly related my thoughts about the restaurant to Milard, so let me tell you too. Anne-Sophie Pic's La Dame de Pic is really a restaurant that those curious about food must visit. Anne-Sophie Pic is not just a "kitchen person" from birth but from before: Four generations of her family have been in the kitchen, so there's cooking coursing through their veins. Their restaurant in the town of Valence now has three Michelin stars, making her one of the first woman chefs to attain the honor. Naturally, her mantle groans under the weight of other awards, while she's also written books about cuisine and opened other restaurants.

Now that Anne-Sophie Pic has branched out into such a wide variety of interests, I don't know whether she'll continue the success she enjoyed with her first forays or whether it'll all break up and start to shrivel – as has been the case with some other French chefs that have opened to the world. Only time will tell...
La Dame de Pic doesn't draw to many foreign customers – it's far more of a "French" restaurant. It's also a good restaurant! The décor is fairly feminine, with pink and white and a lot of wood and leather. Despite a lack of windows, it's not claustrophobic like Bottura's Osteria Francescana in Modena.
"I want my guests to get away from the noise and fracas of the street," Madame Pic says. "I want to create a calm ambiance."

The service is very good, and the unique food is made with care. It's all an endeavor that invites respect. Ultimately, though, they're not the type of dishes that I would choose to return for. I asked for some Ricard as an apéro before the meal, but they didn't have any – these arbitrary restrictions that some restaurants impose because it's "not part of the concept" are not something I find charming or necessary. There were no side plates for the bread (they serve just one type of black bread, although that isn't a problem in itself) and butter, meaning you have to put your greasy knife and bread on top of the white tablecloth. And as you know, even the cleanest tablecloth has germs, so it was a choice that didn't best please me. And it would have been nice if there had been a valet to park the car, because it's a chore trying to find a parking spot in such a crowded area!
Still, they immediately served children with special fare and, like the Jules Verne, they didn't charge them full price. Instead, they charged them a price that was more honest and more reasonable. I wondered to myself whether it was because the boss was a woman...
Merci, Madame Pic.

I'm sure that the appearance of more woman chefs and restaurateurs will have more of us dining out in a more "family-friendly" environment...

# How Did I Direct Traffic At The Washrooms At Georges?

## Georges, Paris

"What is your purpose in coming to Paris?" the passport officer asked me at Charles De Gaulle Airport. "I'm asking myself that as well," I replied.

I really don't know what possessed me to come and spend a weekend in a city that had just witnessed a march by 500,000 people to protest a new labor law, its trains stop working and its daily life ground to a halt. Is an opera, an exhibition and a dinner worth all of this?
The officer laughed. Having received a response in a tone of French that was more literary than that used for the original question, he cut matters short, wished me an enjoyable weekend and furnished my passport with an entry stamp.

The French are huge fans of minimum work and maximum enjoyment such as eating and chatting. Furthermore, they strongly consider this lifestyle as a cornerstone of their overall "human rights" program! Well, maybe they are not that too far wrong on this – who in their right minds would want to work non-stop... except perhaps the Americans and the Germans?

But what about it? Even in tough times, Paris is still Paris! It's even worth coming from afar for the weekend to go the opera, an exhibition and a dinner... Regardless of whether there's a strike or a march!
The Centre Pompidou is not just a cultural center that stages exhibitions, but also a venue for a permanent library and modern art museum. Constructed in memory of a former minister, Georges Pompidou, it opened in 1977.

At first, its ultra-modern architecture engendered hatred and invoked the wrath of the French – just like the Eiffel Tower and the pyramid at the Louvre. Later, the French came to embrace the structure, which became a source of pride – just like the Eiffel Tower and the pyramid at the Louvre.

At the top, there is a restaurant that gives one a glimpse of Paris as far as the eye can see: Georges. Like the pile of steel that is the building, it is also post-modern. It has an enormous façade that is completely glass. The windows might not always be clean, but you can still see Paris in all its majesty, especially when it gleams at night. A person feels good when there.

"May I take your coat?" the beautiful hostess asked.

"No, it's OK. My meds, telephone and whatnot are inside," I said.

The poor girl shot me a look as if to say, "You don't get it, do you, pops?" and said, "I have to do this, monsieur, such measures were put in place after the 'incidents,'" forcing me to sober up to reality in the wake of traumatic events in France. You used to be able to sit down with your coat and overcoat… Where are the days?

Another beautiful girl sporting a miniskirt, high heels and a low-cut dress showed us to our seats. All the girls were like that. It means that it's not only chichi places like L'Avenue that retain such service experts but also the abodes of culture! Our gorgeous and low-cut waitress, however, was not as striking in terms of culture. As we were ordering, I pointed out the Tour St. Jacques and asked, "Mademoiselle, what is the place with the lights across the way?" She looked, but didn't know; "I think it's a church or something," she offered.

The morals of the story?

1. A person needs to be more curious and possess more knowledge about the place in which they work and the job they do!
2. Establishments need to supply broader knowledge to their personnel about the area in which they work and the job they do!

I was the one to supply the information about the monument visible from Georges to the girl!

In return, she brought us wonderful food and provided delightful service. A bottle of 2011 Premier Cru Chablis Les Vaillons went really well with the spicy lobster pasta and Label Rouge salmon.

Before departing, we went to the washroom. Due to the impact of the modern style of interior decorating on the toilet section, it wasn't entirely obvious which was the men's and which was the women's. With the surroundings dusky and the head a bit tipsy, going to the wrong place was entirely possible. As it was, that's exactly what transpired: A young man went into the women's, and when some women followed and saw him, they exited, assuming they'd gone into the wrong washroom. At the time, I was waiting for the missus in a comfortable sofa positioned directly across from the washrooms. I indicated to the ladies who thought they had entered the wrong washroom that they should go back in. Soon after, when I saw more men and women arriving, attempting to deduce which door they should enter, I determined that it was time to roll up my sleeves and get to work. From my position on the sofa, I began directing all comers – "you go here, you there…" Even though my wife returned, I didn't get up, beckoning her to sit next to me: "Join me; it's a good gig."

Long ago – probably a really long time ago – attendants with pitchers of water used to stand on duty outside public washrooms when there was no water (maybe that wasn't so long ago). They would give a pitcher of water from a row in front of the washrooms to those coming to use the facilities. But they would furrow their eyebrow if anyone attempted to pick up any old pitcher – "No, leave that one and take this one," they would say. If anyone asked what difference it made, they would fire back, "That's the way – you wouldn't understand." That's the way they lent an air of importance to themselves and their job. Just like many have done in every age!

So until my wife grabbed me by the arm and led me away, I stood on duty at the washrooms at Georges. And, like all those that used to do it, I did so with great solemnity. "No...No...No, Madame not that way, go in there!" I wish I'd taken another glass of wine and unfurled a tissue in front of myself!

If the police at airport passport control ask me on my next arrival what my purpose in visiting Paris is, I'll say I'm coming to do my duty at the washroom.
Who knows if they'll understand or just say "What a pity... The old man seems to be cultured but he's got a few screws loose."

> " **"What is your purpose in coming to Paris?" the passport officer asked me at Charles De Gaulle Airport. "I'm asking myself that as well", I replied.** "

# The Elegance Of The Maître D' At Blue Hill

## Blue Hill At Stone Barns, New York

The restaurant Blue Hill at Stone Barns is to the north of New York...

First, you come to a village close by with a less-than-comfortable train from Manhattan. After that, you take a cab to get to the restaurant. Altogether, it takes approximately an hour-and-a-half.
Or you could drive to get there, although this might result in lost time depending on the traffic.
Is it worth it?
Absolutely!

The restaurant is on a big farm that once belonged to the Rockefellers ... The complex is now called the Stone Barns Center for Food and Agriculture.
The restaurant Blue Hill (don't confuse it with the Blue Hill in Manhattan) inside the complex was opened in 2004. If I'm not mistaken, we first went there in 2008. I remember saying that the place would earn a great reputation in the future, just like my prediction for Eleven Mad.
I wasn't wrong on either front!
Blue Hill at Stone Barns is now among the best restaurants in the world.

A huge main hall... Tables at a suitable distance from each other... Cozy chairs...
Specially designed plates... Little statuettes for the chips... Everything so delicate and special!
Just like the service!
Plus a maître d'hotel that is polite and runs a tight ship with his team ... Well-informed waiters that never irritate anyone with their service...

Of course, the real talent is hidden in the meals!

Most of what goes into the meals is grown right on the farm – it's all as fresh and organic as can be...

Herbs, vegetables, fruits... Tomatoes... Eggs...

And of course, the meat... Goose, duck, pork, chicken...

What they pick from the garden and what they take from the coop determine the menu. Not you!

You are merely asked if you are allergic to anything, and then you leave the rest to them.

You have what they bring!

But what food! You'll be left polishing off the plate!

Everything is very fresh, and if the cooks are under Dan Barber's watch, then you're in for a feast.

Unless I'm mistaken, it was either in 2009 or in 2010 when we were waiting for the surprise of the day there, that I turned to maître d' and said:

"Our last time here you offered us a 'welcome cocktail.' Are you not offering it anymore?"

"Sir, you must be mistaken; we have never served such a cocktail!"

Man, I recall drinking a glass of champagne or sparkling wine.

I didn't say anything, but I started eating my meal with great disappointment.

Anyway, everything went well; we ate a delicious and pleasant meal.

Toward the end, we got thinking about a spot of Château d'Yquem to be accompanied by dessert.

My son, however, drew attention to the fact that this little bottle would be enough for a round-trip journey to London!

I paid no attention! "We'll at least have a glass," I said as I ordered the drink!

Being a part of our little argument on the "welcome cocktail" at the beginning of the meal, the maître d' himself brought a little bottle of d'Yquem.

Meanwhile, my wife said: "Not for me – it's too much." Displaying solidarity with her mother-in-law, my daughter-in-law proffered an excuse, choosing instead to make sacrifices for the family budget. My son and I paid them no heed. But I've always wondered if it would have been possible to survive financially without these women!

Anyway, we took a sip of our wine. The maître d' asked,

"How did you find it, sir?"

"Perfect enough to make us lose ourselves," I said as if I was a dab hand at tasting wines!

Pleased, the maître d' left the bottle of wine on the table and departed.

We liked it a lot, but we faced the prospect of hitchhiking back to New York if we were to drink another glass. Just like cats yearning for a morsel of food, we gazed longingly at the wine... But then came the maître d', who had already been observing us from the corner of his eye, and poured the rest of the little bottle into our glasses!

While we were leaving the table, the waiter whispered to my son: "Wouldn't you know it? Somehow or other this bottle looks like it's going to disappear." He offered the rest of the d'Yquem, which, while tiny, would cost at least 50 dollars!

My wife and daughter-in-law couldn't pass up this opportunity!

Instead of a "welcome cocktail," we were served a more expensive "one for the road."

No one ever gets ahead of the other by standing still!

The same goes for an artist...

Or a doctor...

Or a restaurant...

There is a reason behind any success!

# A Pastry For Some, A Pasting For Others From Rita Hayworth

## Le Pavillon Eden Roc, Cap D'antibes

It's a warm summer night, and out among the diners on the hotel terrace is a beautiful and famous woman, sitting alone. At another table is an elegant man, also eating alone. André Sella, the hotel's owner, knows them both. First he heads to the man's table, and then to the woman's...

"Why are you guys eating on your own? Wouldn't you like to dine together and enjoy such a beautiful evening?" he asks them both.

Both parties heed his suggestion, and the man draws a chair up at the woman's table.

The move first fosters love and, ultimately, marriage.

This time, the young, beautiful and famous woman moves in with the wealthy man who joined her at her table. She spends her time making honey pastries for her new beau.

The woman was none other than the sex bomb of the age, Rita Hayworth. The man, meanwhile, was none other than the richest of the rich, Ali Khan.

The place where they met was the famous Eden Roc hotel in Cap d'Antibes.

As in any Hollywood film, the meeting of the couple concluded with a happy ending. There was one person, however, who got the short end of the stick in this otherwise joyous case of affairs – an individual that just happens to be a friend of mine. He was studying dentistry at the Sorbonne and came to Antibes for his internship in the summer.

He also knew where the young and beautiful Rita was staying; occasionally, he would secretly climb the wall and watch her surreptitiously as she swam in the pool. One day, while standing as a sentinel in his duty, he was grabbed by the scruff of the neck by one of her bodyguards.

"Hey handsome, what do you think you're doing here?"

Caught unprepared, my friend stammered "I... I... I... what am I doing here?" as the bodyguards brought him down and laid into him, divesting him of two of his teeth for good measure.

The pursuit of Rita resulted in a honey pastry for one of her suitors and a pasting for the other...

The friend in dentistry got to welcome himself as his first customer for his first operation...

The Hôtel du Cap-Eden-Roc is a place that the planet's finite number of rich people, Hollywood stars and famous artists absolutely love, and the same goes for me. If I knew I wouldn't stick out like a sore thumb among all those famous people, I'd like to go there for a week for some R&R after seriously (and I mean seriously) saving up all my pennies.

Located in a magnificent garden, the place was converted from a traditional mansion into a hotel. The mansion was originally commissioned by Le Figaro's owner, Auguste de Villemessant, and christened Villa Soleil at its inception. Assorted writers and painters found sanctuary here, and the villa was soon bursting at the gills with artists. In 1889, Antoine Sella bought the edifice and converted it into a hotel. From that date on, everyone who's enjoyed some fame and wealth, from Bernard Shaw to Pablo Picasso and from Marc Chagall to the Duke of Windsor, has beaten a path to its door. The duke, in fact, even came and sequestered himself here after abdicating the British thrown for the sake of his lover (naturally, he shared his seclusion with her). And they say Chagall stayed without ever paying his bill, finally making and signing a drawing that he left at the reception.

After leaving the mansion and passing through the expansive and peaceful garden (while promenading through it, one would be forgiven for reckoning they are either in Versailles or at the Summer Palace in Saint Petersburg), one arrives at the seashore – that's where the restaurant is. Because the "pavilion" was added subsequently, it doesn't architecturally match the complex's main building. And from your seat, you're likely to feel as if you're dining on the bridge of a vessel as its plies the deep-blue waters of the Mediterranean. Right below is the beach, while there's also a small infinity pool. The sea, meanwhile, is set off with buoys that are preceded by netting to protect some of the more delicate customers from the ill intentions of any jellyfish. Naturally, the price of a hotel that extends such attention to its customers, along with its restaurant, is bound to be high.

They also say that one day, when Picasso was dining there, he announced during an interlude of joy that he would "draw the menu."

"But Monsieur, it would be a great honor, but how would we ever recover, I mean, how much would that be?" they asked fearfully.

"Just give me a pen, paper and some ink; I don't want any noise," he responded, the Maître D' related to us.

I felt compelled to jump in at this anecdote:

"Where do you get your fish from?" I asked; nothing else came to mind – especially as my expensive sea bass could hardly be depicted as scrumptious.

"From there!" he exclaimed, indicating the sea with his hand.

"Really, instead of getting them from here, wouldn't it just be better to import them from a fish farm in the Aegean?" I was about to say, only to recall my friend who was divested of his teeth just a few steps away. Instead, I kept mum.

"What's for dessert?" I chose to ask instead.

The only damage incurred was to my wallet and sugar levels...

# In Pursuit Of Stolen Pride

## Bernardin, New York

The young man came home one evening to find his wife bawling her eyes out. He embraced and kissed her, and then asked why she was crying.

"I put the basil out on the balcony to get some fresh air. When the doorman Harun saw it, would you believe what he said? 'Is that the plant you stole from number 10?' I was thrown for an absolute loop... I subjected him to the hairdryer treatment – 'What the hell are you saying? Why would I steal someone else's plant? Are you crazy?' – but I couldn't get the point across to him. He just went and drove me crazy: 'You stole it, you stole it! I know it!' he said."

"You mean the plant that I got, no?"

"Of course that one."

The young man got a rush of blood to the head. It was all completely ridiculous. As he was bringing the basil home, an elderly woman turned to him on the metro and sighed: "Well done, my son. Young men these days are tied to their home just like women. Were men like that in our day?"

The young man was unable to determine whether the old woman was complimenting him or longing for the men of yesteryear...

He took a deep breath in front of the doorman's place and then shouted at the top of his lungs.

There was no response from the doorman.

Still, the young man said, "Can you prove that we stole the plant?"

The doorman, who had hitherto been listening silently, responded immediately this time:

"Can you prove that you didn't?"

Like us, he too knew that there were two possible avenues in the pursuit of justice:
* The use of civilized and legal paths;
* The use of brute force.

The young man was a civilized, white-collar worker. Confronted by the prospect of the doorman, who was sporting 20 extra kilos in girth and 20 extra centimeters in height, he naturally selected the civilized path, opting to speak with the apartment manager. He might be able to punish the doorman for his behavior.

The apartment manager had finished his dinner and was watching a soap opera on TV. Not wanting to take up too much of his time, he relayed the issue immediately. Without diverting his attention from the screen, the manager responded:

"I see, I see. Let's hear what the doorman has to say tomorrow."

It was as if he was a criminal judge!

He left the manager to his soap opera. He ran to the neighborhood police station. They were bound to provide some form of justice.

It was his first time coming to a police station. At the counter was a red-faced, rotund and elderly officer peeling an apple. In the back room, another officer observed the newcomer while fiddling with a radio in his hand. Which one to ask? There was someone in front of him, but all his attention had been invested in the apple. The other officer was looking at him but was in the back room. Finally, the officer with the apple raised his head:

"Yes?"

"Sir, I've come to a police station for the first time."

"You're certainly not the first person to come at this late hour…"

The man wasn't sure how to respond. "My wife…" he stuttered.

"You killed your wife?"

The young man managed to finally relay the issue at length.

"Go in – give your statement to the guy there!"

The young man went in… Who knows what state he was in, because when he went in, "the guy in there" turned off the radio and said, "Sit down."

"I can't sit; I'm late," the man pleaded.

"Man, why did you come here then? If you had something to do, you shouldn't have come!" the officer retorted.

The young man sat down. "So if you didn't want to, why did you sit down?" the officer's face appeared to say this time, only for him to actually utter, "So tell me what's going on."

He related the issue at length once more.

"Here's the thing I don't get," the officer said when the young man had finished. "If that guy's plant was stolen, why have you come to complain instead of him?"

"Sir, there is no stolen plant! What's been stolen is pride. The pride of me and my wife! We've been slandered, and I'm trying to do something about this injustice!" the young man exclaimed.

The officer shook his head from side to side, seemingly wondering what they had done to merit such a visit. As he was entering the statement in the computer, the older policeman entered and placed his hand on the young man's shoulder.

"Look, champ," he said. "You look like a good guy, but you don't know anything about life yet. We've been run off our feet since the morning, and we've had to deal with stuff like you wouldn't believe. But now you're here, wailing that you didn't steal some plant. You're exhausting us too. How much does this plant cost? Look, people are dying every day. There are so many problems in the world, but are we going to drop everything and deal with your plant? If you really want to, give a statement, but if you ask me, you're better off not bothering. Go home, go to bed and don't get us involved because nothing's going to come of it."

The young man exited the station without finding his justice.

He took a breath of the fresh air.

Apparently, as humanity's problems grew, mankind's values diminished. Apparently, injustice had become ubiquitous – only opposing it was deemed extraordinary.

Like the young man, many of us are quite sensitive on some topics – myself included. Something that others don't care about much might be of extreme importance to me. One such topic is the fairness of the attention shown to the patrons of restaurants. I pay close attention to whether there is equality in the way the chef or restaurant manager wanders among the tables after a meal. Some people don't pay this much thought, but I do. Attention must be paid to every customer, not just to some! If that doesn't happen, no one can speak of any fairness!

Bernardin is a restaurant with three Michelin stars in New York that largely offers a seafood menu. I went with my wife and my son sometime in the 1990s. The décor was out of style, but the tables were spread out enough that the sitting arrangement was comfortable. We sampled some great fish, but for what? Toward the end of the meal, a thin and elegant lady, together with a gentleman, walked among "some" tables, engaging in a bit of chit-chat. As far I could tell, they were people that were well-known in the world of wining and dining, but I didn't bother to find out then, and I still haven't today. The tables that they visited were probably those of patrons that frequently came to the restaurant. There's nothing wrong with them going to talk to them, but what had the rest of us done wrong? I suppose that they didn't show us the same attention because they didn't know us. But they couldn't even come to us and the other tables and spare us a simple "Hi, how are you?" – a phrase that never goes a minute without being pronounced somewhere in America. No, they failed to act fairly toward their customers.

I never went to Bernardin again. Did I steer clear of it because I didn't like the food? Because it was too expensive? Absolutely not! I didn't go because I couldn't find what I wanted: attention and fairness… I didn't go because I wouldn't consent to such treatment…

Nefes Gezgin. Photo by margaarfarm business site

# Why Did Marilyn Monroe Kiss My Father?

## Gaonnuri, New York

My father fought in the Korean War as the commander of an artillery unit.

Before going to Korea, he took me along with him for six months of exercises in a mountainous area of İzmir. I wasn't even in primary school yet. Probably the only civilian in the whole unit, I stayed in my father's tent. I spent the whole day running and playing in the bush, which pervaded the whole place with the scent of thyme.

But there are two events that happened to me that I can't forget:

The first was when I really needed to go use the facilities but the orderly who was taking care of me wasn't around… I opened the flat to the big tent where my father was conducting a briefing with American officers and said, "Daddy, I need to poop!" Everyone was rolling on the floor, laughing at this blond-haired rascal with short pants and chubby legs. The briefing was duly adjourned for a "poo break."

The second was when they fastened a banner about 50 or 60 meters behind a plane for target practice by the artillery. Naturally, it was a pretty risky undertaking for the plane and pilot. What's worse, though, is that one time my father put me in the target plane and hit the mark while I was airborne with the pilot!
He was a really good artillery officer who showcased his abilities in Korea, winning a medal of excellence. My mother, however, was not of the opinion that he was much of a father. When she heard about this escapade, she took me back and never forgave him!

To raise the morale of the soldiers in Korea, they would bring famous stars from the States for appearances. There was one time that the most spellbinding star of them all, Marilyn Monroe, also joined the fray, putting in a performance for the soldiers with her steamy, sexy voice. (You would have heard the same song years later when she sang it for President JFK on his birthday.) During her set in Korea, she sang JJohnny is the boy for me, which was famous at the time.

After the concert, they introduced the famous star to all the commanders. MM proceeded her way up the line, shaking the officers' hands one by one until she reached my father... My dad bent down toward her ear and, riffing on her song, whispered, "Marilyn is the girl for me."

Not expecting such improvisation, the legendary singer was first taken aback before she laughed, hugging and kissing my father.

There is a Korean restaurant called Gaonnuri at the top of a skyscraper in Manhattan. When the lights come on at night and you get a chance to survey the forest of skyscrapers, it's wonderful – and delicious – to sample typical Korean dishes, all while engaging in a little bit of nostalgia about your father's exploits in Korea.

> **"** After the concert, they introduced the famous star to all the commanders. MM proceeded her way up the line, shaking the officers' hands one by one until she reached my father... My dad bent down toward her ear and, riffing on her song, whispered, "Marilyn is the girl for me." **"**

# My Adventure With Caviar Risotto At Osteria Francescana

## Osteria Francescana, Modena

I was aware of Massimo Bottura, the owner of Osteria Francescana and one of the globe's best and most charismatic chefs.

He's a master of his craft and someone who really knows the marketing side of the game.

His Osteria Francescana in Modena was listed first on the list of 50 Best Restaurants in 2016 and second the following year.

Bottura was a chef who created food that was a work of art by channeling an inner artistic inspiration. He was also a kitchen revolutionary who married the best of his ingredients and techniques with art to create food.

He was a modern chef who was aware of the need to look to the future while also remaining keenly aware of the importance of looking into the rear-view mirror, recommending that the journey set off from grandma's recipes – not for the sake of a nostalgic trip down memory lane, but as a learning exercise to stimulate creativity.

I already knew all of this. But as I was perusing a parmigiano factory in Modena, I met a completely different side of the maestro – to the point that I can say I only met Bottura then and there. This side of the maestro was the one that unites his charity and commercial pragmatism, as well as the one that unites his humanity and productive and effective solutions to a societal problem.

Modena was rocked by a large earthquake in May 2012. The cheese storages belonging to parmigiano producers suffered damage to the tune of between 100 and 200 million euros. (It should not be a shock to you that the discrepancy stems from the fact the figures are furnished by Italian sources). Everyone rolled up their sleeves to heal the wounds from the earthquake, including Bottura – with all his creativity – by creating a recipe that would also increase the use of parmigiano. Following a little home experiment, the maestro changed the famous cacio e pepe dish, which is made with spaghetti and pecorino cheese, substituting parmigiano for the ricotta and rice for the spaghetti. But that wasn't all: Bottura then reshaped this pasta dish into a pizza format. Creating a hit, the updated dish also fostered a significant increase in parmigiano consumption. Thanks to an announcement on social media, everyone in Italy sat down to eat this meal at 8 o'clock on the evening of 27 October.

The campaign was a success, as the consumption of parmigiano went through the roof, compensating for the damages incurred by the producers. Modena, in turn, applauded Bottura.

We were looking at Google Maps while wandering the narrow streets of Modena. While searching for the town's famous Zelmira restaurant, Bottura's Osteria Francescana materialized right in front of us? People were taking photos in front of the door, and when in Modena, do as the Modenans do.

But while taking the photo of my wife and son, my viewfinder couldn't help but spy a group from the restaurant in work attire, kicking around a ball as they waited for the dinner rush. Given the trial that just walking on some of the old cobblestones is, I was immediately struck by the ball control of one of the youth. I had half a mind to go over and offer him a position in the starting XI for my club's midfield, only to be stopped by entreaties from my wife and son that we were running late for Zelmira and running the risk of incurring a no-show penalty.

"I hope these guys straighten themselves out and wash up before they head inside," my wife said as we ventured in. And so it was that the passion for calcio among Bottura and his team helped me meet him once more.

We finally headed to Bottura's restaurant for lunch. The famous chef himself was not in evidence, but his restaurant is naturally his calling card, and I certainly saw that. Our son had come all the way from San Francisco to join us for this meal. Bottura himself, unfortunately, was in New York, but sous chefs Davide di Fabio and Takaiko Kondo had picked up the baton in his absence. Our server, meanwhile, was Denis Bretta, whom I recognized from Bottura's commercials.

The amuse-bouches presented before us consisted of fish and chips, eel and rabbit macaroons – all interesting experiments.

For an appetizer, my wife opted for the dish intriguingly named "an eel swimming up the Po river," while my son went for the Code mare nostrum, to be accompanied by a Fonte Canale 2015. For my part, I asked for the Croccantino of foie gras. I can honestly say that my foie gras, which was filled with caramelized hazelnuts and walnuts and balanced out with balsamic vinegar, was the most original and delicious I've ever had. In this, it was impossible not to recognize the signature of Bottura's creativity.

In between, they offered spoonfuls of leeks in cream and parmigiano.

For an entrée, my wife selected the "Lobster with double sauces, both acidic and sweet" while my son chose the suckling pig with a Primitivo di Manduria, Gianfranco Fino 2014 ES – a red Puglia wine.

For my entrée, I moved in for the "gray and black rice with Oscietra Royal Caviar." I had dined on Risotto di Mare in 2015 at the Istanbul restaurant opened by Bottura, and although the concoction of rice, pasta and seafood isn't normally my cup of tea, I enjoyed it.

This time, I elected to try the risotto caviar. Taking a forkful of grey and black rice with risotto, I told Denis, "This fish smells funny."

"That's because it was cooked with oysters," came the reply.

"But it doesn't say that on the menu," would have been my reply if I hadn't chosen to instead just eat my meal. Try as I might, though, I could only get through half of it before throwing in the towel. No one asked either why I had only eaten half my meal at such a famous kitchen.

For dessert it was tiramisu, although I can say that I've had better ones in Italy before. The petit fours that came with the coffee were also fairly ordinary.

But the thing that wasn't ordinary was what happened to me in the evening: terrible food poisoning that left me quite the worse for wear both that evening and the following two days. To avoid public humiliation as a result of my condition, the whole family banded together to help. And although we had seats in front of the orchestra pit at the Luciano Pavarotti Theater for Soirée Pepita, I had to observe proceedings from a more inexpensive box on the top floor given its closer proximity to the gents' room. The same scene played out the following evening in Parma during the Victorija Mullova recital.

But despite all our precautions, we failed to achieve maximum success. If my wife hadn't been with me and around to occasionally "clean up," I wouldn't have been worthy of even feeling shame toward the amiable Luca at Modena's Cervetta 5 Hotel or to Vittorio, who oversaw all of our events with aplomb and kindness at Parma's Palazzo Della Rosa. Naturally, I'm not one to suggest that I fell ill because of such a famous restaurant as the Osteria Francescana (even if it has fallen from first to second in the world rankings). That would hardly be believable, and as someone who studied law, I also know it's not fair to make such a claim in the absence of any concrete evidence. Still, there's no denying my two days of trial and tribulation, as well as the smell of fish that was always welling at the top of my throat.

With its hall of five tables, the Osteria Francescana fits the notion of an "osteria." But the other definitions that go with the term, such as being simple or inexpensive, are most certainly not in evidence. And unlike the establishment that it lost its number-one spot to, Eleven Mad, it doesn't quite fit the bill of being "a true restaurant." Instead, it would probably be more appropriate to describe the place as "Bottura's showroom." As it is, Bottura himself calls his establishment a "laboratory of ideas."

But whether it's a showroom or a laboratory, the five-table hall was closed to the outside and fairly claustrophobic. The ground was covered in a brown, wall-to-wall factory-made carpet, while the walls sported nothing more than a coat of dark-colored latex paint and some portraits of Edith Piaff. The combination of the scents of the carpet, food, alcohol and exhaled breath made the small, five-table hall feel remarkably airless. And it wouldn't be an exaggeration to suggest that even if the boss is a fan of the slow food movement, the restaurant's stale air was enough to have us down our fare quickly and depart.

I should, however, touch on why the Istanbul location of Signor Bottura, who gives off an air of not only creativity, sensitivity and love for the arts but also that of a successful businessman, failed to succeed. In 2015, Signor Bottura opened a location in Istanbul called Ristorante Italia di Massimo Bottura, only to close soon after.

I inquired with Daniele, who had worked there as the Maître D' before moving onto Il Riccio Bodrum. "The location was bad – it looked onto the highway."

But that's partly true and partly false. It's true because Bottura opened the place in a mall and false because there were a number of successful restaurants in that very shopping center, including some that possess a favorable international reputation. More to the point, the restaurant boasted a spacious balcony and the ostensible highway was an avenue heading toward the Bosphorus bridge. And there certainly wasn't that much space in Modena.

I asked the same question this time to Denis at the Francescana. "People in Istanbul weren't yet ready," he said in summary of the situation.

That, too, is partly true and partly false. It's true because, like the example of Hakkasan, it's a fact that restaurants that tend to implement a different pricing policy in comparison to the standard in Istanbul encounter more difficulties after opening. It's false because Istanbul does feature a customer segment that is prepared to pay top dollar to keep restaurants that "respect the customer" in business. As a matter of fact, it's not always easy to find a place at restaurants in Istanbul that are even more expensive. Likewise, the customers who are willing to go to such places have the means to frequent places around the world that are even more expensive. A quick glance at social media provides sufficient evidence in that direction. In my opinion, Ristorante di Bottura failed to survive in Istanbul due to an incorrect and inadequate feasibility plan. It's not that the Istanbul clientele wasn't ready, it is that the investor himself failed to conduct a sufficient feasibility study or make the correct strategic choices, instead entering the market unprepared.

Let me give an example: I went to the restaurant one evening for an event organized by the Istanbul Rotary Club. Ristorante di Bottura had organized a six-course tasting menu centered on two main dishes: Baccalà e ceci (Salted codfish) and Guancia all'aceto Balsamico (Beef cheek in balsamic sauce). I would never lend credence to the populist notion that the chef should make concessions on his signature dishes and prepare a menu with fare in the style "demanded by customers." But "making concessions to customers" is one thing and "respecting customers" – and carving out an according commercial niche – is another. Istanbul is one of the few metropoles that boasts fish that is always multifarious, always delicious and always fresh. As such, offering frozen cod to a customer segment that is used to something fresh just because it's on the menu in Modena is nothing but a slight to your clientele.

Similarly, the beef cheek was cooked with the "sous vide" technique, which ensures meat and fish are soft, but, I ask you, do you want your food to be soft, hard, spicy, sweet et cetera, or do you want it to be "delicious?" I know that there are at least a dozen restaurants in Istanbul, particularly Niso Adato's Şans restaurant, that can cook beef cheek for five or six hours so that it's both soft and delicious. If you're going to serve meat with a plastic taste at such an exorbitant price to a customer segment that's used to the aforementioned quality, it suggests, in a nutshell, that you didn't do enough homework when coming here, that you're only resting on the laurels of your name and that you assumed "they'll like whatever I tell them to."
This result is unfortunate for someone like Bottura, given how much he cares about vision.
Returning to Modena, I'd say that, personally, I expect a true kitchen revolutionary and artist like Bottura to pursue a new challenge. Bottura needs to leave behind the laboratory and showroom concept that has been a proven success and make a name for himself among "real restaurants" like Eleven Mad, Heston Blumenthal, Blue Hill or Apicius. His accumulation of experience, dynamism and maturity present the ideal environment for this kind of venture.
I wouldn't want to see him insist on the laboratory concept, but if he did, it wouldn't be a surprise to see new up-and-coming geniuses steal his place near the top of the top restaurants list...

# The Little Blond Boy

## Ristorante Nino, Rome

Primary school had yet to even start for the cute, blond boy.

His parents had split up. Of course, they loved him a lot, but they didn't have a whole lot of time to take him on outings. Still, from time to time, his uncle would take him and his brother out to a football match.

One time, his uncle took him to an international equestrian event; he took a seat in the stands, sporting a bib featuring a bird with outstretched wings. He watched excitedly as the horses and their riders cleared the obstacles. Desperate for the riders from his own national team to win, he couldn't help himself when a major foreign contender prepared to negotiate the course.

"I hope your horse breaks a leg," he blurted out.

His uncle was greatly perturbed by the exclamation. "Look," he said. "Whether you're competing or watching, what's important is fair play. After all, isn't that the way it's supposed to be in life, too? Cheer for your side, pray for their success, but don't desire something bad to happen to someone else.

"That's not sporting in any way, shape or form!"

The boy had learnt his lesson on gentlemanly conduct, sportsmanship and honesty. He understood what he had done wrong, regretted his ill wishes and, while I didn't see it, might even have shed a tear or two.

The little blond boy grew up, grabbed life by the horns and went to matches, screaming his head off, but never again wishing ill upon the opposing team.

Later, he got on in years – he stopped going to the stadium but would watch matches on TV instead. With this transition, there was no more screaming and shouting, but just silent observation of the screen instead. His new demeanor had not escaped the notice of his wife.

"Back in the day you couldn't sit still during a match. In fact, you'd take advantage of every opportunity to have another drink," she said. "What's become of you?"

What became of him? The years mellowed him out and matured him. There's nothing else to it!

It's no different with restaurants. In the normal order of things, they first open with great expectations; in the beginning of their new life, they sometimes err as they look to grow accustomed to their surroundings. During this time, they make a lot of mistakes. After that comes the years of survival and getting on with life. In the merciless world of competition, they pick fights, defend themselves and strive to get a step ahead of their rivals. During this period, some manage to survive, while others are left by the wayside and forced to close up shop.

For those that do survive, they now find themselves in the age of maturity. They're sure of themselves, calm and dignified as they lead a respectable and sedate existence.

Ristorante Nino belongs in this category.

Located in the heart of Rome, it serves Florentine cuisine. As you enter, you are greeted by wood-paneled walls, old-style tables and chairs and lamps from another era. It's sedate, calm and established... If, by chance, you enjoy such surroundings, you'll immediately feel at home. But is it only the décor? The staff also blend in with the surroundings, as they've advanced in years themselves. They're people who have lived, sussed out, witnessed and gone through life.

"How long has this place been here?" I asked.

"Since 1934," the elderly waiter informed me.

I wasn't surprised. I really appreciated the place's air of maturity, while my food was also quite good. Its artichokes in olive oil were extraordinary, while the ribollita is naturally a specialty. However, despite Nino being a purveyor of Florentine cuisine, its "Bistecca alla fiorentina" wasn't as good as I expected.

But I ask you this: Is it fair and right to expect those that have managed to reach a ripe old age to still do everything perfectly?

“Look”, he said. “Whether you're competing or watching, what's important is fair play. After all, isn't that the way it's supposed to be in life, too?”

# The Restaurant Of The Night Of Horror

## Max, Auburn (California)

When I just made out the sign for the rest area, I shivered at the excitement of soon reuniting with my newfound lover.

It was around 8 in the evening. It was pitch dark. It was impossible to see anything because of the blizzard which, needless to say, made everything freezing cold. The roads were icy. People were rushing to do their business and get back to their cars.

The parking lot was full. "I'll let you out in front of the door, park the car and come," said my son, who was driving. I got out gingerly to avoid slipping and falling. I wanted to run to the object of my desire but refrained from doing so to avoid ending up in a bad situation.

My strength, however, escaped me at the door, and I let it all out before I made it to the latest love of my life, the bathroom!

I had been suffering from terrible diarrhea for the past three days. I couldn't eat, drink or leave the bathroom. I had lost more than three kilos already. We had been vacationing at my son and daughter-in-law's cabin in Tahoe for a week and were returning to San Francisco. We made a tour of all the rest areas along the way, continuing on again after I explored the nether regions of the bathrooms.

San Francisco was just three to five hours away, but there was such crazy traffic that there was almost no movement on the two-lane mountain roads or the highway. Because of Christmas and New Year's, people headed to their winter had flocked to hotels. We had taken precautions and even thought we would be able to drive all night. That, thankfully, was what we did, because we later learned that some had only managed to complete the drive in 10 hours, rather than the normal three to five.

It was the first time I had soiled myself, and I was a mess. My wife came to my aid with fresh undergarments and pants, taking me to a stall in the gents' room under the suspicious gazes of other patrons. The floor was wet and muddy. The cold almost froze your breath. I didn't even have the strength to stand. I felt dizzy and later on learned that my blood pressure had dropped to around 5. There was no place to sit; I could have fainted at any minute without the hope of ever getting up. All I can remember saying is, "Is there anybody else waiting outside the stall? I don't want to keep them waiting."

She cleaned me up and redressed me, while she and my son carried me to the car. In the second car, my daughter-in-law was trying to control her two little kids, who had grown bored of watching their favorite cartoon during the long journey in the dark. They were acting out and crying in their seats. My son immediately gave me an energy drink. It would have been better to have a glass of red wine in a setting that featured snow-covered pine trees overlooking a fast-flowing creek, but I didn't even have the strength for a glass of water. I collapsed into my seat. They strapped on my seat belt, and we began moving.

When we arrived at the Holiday Inn in Auburn, they suggested I go to bed and feed me with room service. I declined the offer; I just had to see the restaurant of the facility after a night of excitement. Thankfully, the restaurant, Max's, was on the same floor of our rooms, so I was able to practically crawl there.

Max's was a typical inn diner. It's a small, charming restaurant that caters to hungry masses if that's what you were looking for – and almost everyone who came there had the same purpose! It offered the epitome of American cuisine... Giant burgers, pizzas, salads that included chicken, cheese, ham, bacon and sausages more than vegetables, noodles filled with meat more than soup, beverages with tons of sugar and ice cream with toppings... I wanted none of it. I wouldn't have wanted them even if I had been healthy. I asked for plain macaroni and yoghurt. In return, I got a slightly creamy and cheesy macaroni and fruit-flavored yoghurt.

Max's is a small, cute restaurant fit for those looking to fill their stomachs. But it means so much more to me because it's a restaurant that fed me and got me on my feet during that night of torment.

On my next trip to Tahoe, I will surely visit it and salute this friend who was with me in my hour of need. And why not – I may even have a cheeseburger and an apple juice too...

# Have You Every Missed The Ballet For A Meal?

## Relais Plaza, Paris

Have you ever missed the ballet for a meal? It happened to us, unfortunately!

But is it appropriate to say "unfortunately?" I don't really know… Let me tell the story, and then you can decide:

I had gotten tickets to the Para-ll-elle ballet performance at the Théâtre Des Champs Elysées in the front row. The ballet was set to start at 8.30 p.m., and we had arrived there by 6. We perused the Triangle d'Or (The Triangle of Gold), engaged in a spot of window-shopping at the fashion houses on Avenue Montaigne and did some people-watching on the off chance we'd see someone we knew…

Somewhat tuckered out, we decided to head for a restaurant, both to kill some time and to recharge. There are plenty of restaurants that I know in the vicinity – some which I like, and some which I don't.

The closest to the theater is the Bar de l'Entracte, sitting right across from it. Its name ("theater intermission") is appropriate for the environs and cute to boot.

On the same side as the theater a little further along is the more popular L'Avenue. The place is one that models in the area particularly frequent for lunch – meaning attention from men is always in abundance. Since not all the models are women, there is no lack of male models and their admirers either. From the greeter at the door to the servers inside, all the female personnel are specially selected gorgeous women – who effectively issue a challenge to the models coming for lunch. As for the male personnel, there's no one who isn't handsome and beautiful! Altogether, L'Avenue is an establishment that's posh, young and modern with a bit of swagger.

Coming back from the Montaigne toward the George V, Chez Francis, which takes up the whole corner, is a great place for people looking for a quick bite rather than a bigger meal. What's more, it's in a great location overlooking the square, the Seine and the Eiffel Tower. (In Paris, the city of cafés, my favorites are the Francis and the Au Bord de Seine by Châtelet, Café de l'Art at the entrance to Boul'mich and Les Deux Magots in Saint Germain Des Pres.)

If you don't go for Chez Francis on your return, there's a fish restaurant that'll come up ahead: Marius et Janette. The seafood is great, the waiters are not! A bit further on the left is Le Cinq, a Four Seasons restaurant with three Michelin stars. Rue Marbeuf on the right, meanwhile, is basically a street with restaurants. Once upon a time, there were a number of good options here, but simpler and more touristic establishments later gained predominance.

Right at the end of the theater, there are two restaurants on the ground floor of the famous Plaza Athenée. The first, Alain Ducasse, is geared more toward those that enjoy "fine dining," the rich who are curious about what a place with three Michelin stars is like, dirty old men who spare no expense to impress young ladies and diners who have the benefit of charging everything to a company expense account. It is highly recommended that you make a reservation well in advance. Still, I once went a day before a lunch to reserve a table and noticed plenty of empty tables!

The other restaurant, Relais Plaza, is also chic and expensive, but has slightly less swagger. That's where we went, at 7 o'clock – still an hour and a half before the start of the ballet! We wined and dined without a care and had a long chat with the lobby manager, who turned out to be an acquaintance. Our fare was without question both delicious and beautifully presented. For a restaurant of this standard and at this price, however, I see such matters as par for the course, so I shan't dwell on them, but I do want to touch on one nuance: the flavor of the sauce that came with the sea bass. Along the Aegean and the Mediterranean, they simply apply garlic, lemon, parsley and olive oil to grilled sea bass. After all, when you're eating free fish, you don't need much else. That's why I first expressed disdain for the sauce at the Plaza, but I later realized that its taste was worth writing home about. Perhaps the fact that the fennel sauce put one in the mood for rakı also played a role, but who knows

At 8.15, we departed the restaurant and approached the door of the theater next door.
"Jacket!" a rude security guard at the door barked.
"What about the jacket?"
"Open the front of your jacket!"

After comprehending the reason for the order, we were ushered into a completely empty foyer! With nary a chance to even express our surprise at the sight, a more convivial guard approached, informing us that we had come late, that the show had already started and that because there was no intermission, we would only be permitted into the gallery.

"But it's only 8.20! How could it have started?" we said, only to be confronted with the reality printed on our ticket: apparently the ballet started at 8, but I had kept thinking it was 8.30!
Oh this elderliness! I wouldn't recommend it to anyone...

We ascended to the gallery with the elevator... The Théâtre Des Champs Elysées is extremely chic and one of my favorite concert halls in Paris. It was constructed with the aim of creating an alternative to the traditional players of the Paris opera and especially to promote modern music, dance and opera. Boasting an Art Deco architectural style, the hall played host to the Russian ballet's world premiere of Stravinsky's Rite of Spring ballet. The place known as the gallery is on the top floor and consists of boxes above the fourth balcony. We entered a box with an open door, employing our powers of manual dexterity to find some seats in the dark. They called the place a box, but they were such strange cells that even from the seats at the very front, it was impossible to see a third of the stage! You could only view what was happening on the remainder of the stage.

Regardless, it was enough for us! You'll appreciate that paying a pretty penny for seats right in front of the orchestra pit, arriving at the location hours in advance only to come late for the show and being forced to perch in the balcony is not something just anyone would be able to accomplish. But the two-thirds of the ballet performance that we were able to view wiped away our disappointment… Not because it was really good, but because we hadn't been forced to view an act of the performance after coming late! It was a two-person ballet… I've always liked duets in ballet, but if the whole performance just consists of two people, if one act is solely devoted to movements without music and if the only external audible sound is exclusively directed at French speakers – complete with literary codes such as "you are the home, I am the shelter" and "the thing between us is everything" that are frighteningly difficult to parse after two glasses of wine – then it's not an easy task to digest such a performance.

It the end, it's not one I enjoyed!
That's why I asked: "When you miss the complete ballet, should you bemoan the matter, or be content?"

> " At 8.15, we departed
> the restaurant and approached
> the door of the theater next door.
> "Jacket!" a rude security guard at
> the door barked.
> "What about the jacket?"
> "Open the front of your jacket!" "

Photo by Mustafa Bayram

# Von Karajan And Per Se

## Per Se, New York

They say that Herbert von Karajan was one of the most famous and popular orchestral conductors to have ever walked the earth.

With a great physique, he also boasted a striking visage that turned the heads of ladies.
His greying hair was also coiffed and combed with great care and attention. I believe his hair was specially lacquered to fly all over the place as he expended extreme energy while conducting the orchestra.
He never had any notes in front of him...

Occasionally, he would have a wand in his hand, but not in general...
His eyes were almost always closed.
When the symphony started, the audience was listening to the music, but their attention was directed all at the maestro as they beheld this charismatic artist with eyes closed and coiffed hair flying about, tearing himself to pieces as he dove left and right conducting the famous orchestra, all without the aid of notes. The maestro was a feast not only for the ears but also the eyes.

I've heard his own voice. (But don't think that I'm a geriatric peer of his; I'm as much a senior as Bill Clinton is.) No, he said this in a documentary: "The 12 concerts that I gave in Tokyo were made into a film. About 18-20 million people watched each concert on TV. But in a concert hall, you can only perform for 3,000 people at most. That's when I came to understand the importance of visuality in inculcating a love of music."

After the Tokyo concert series, they started making "concert films," taking von Karajan's lead. But this new undertaking was something beyond the mere broadcast of concerts. Concert productions are generally filmed in an empty hall; after the obligatory technical work on the raw images and sound, the footage is presented to an audience. Von Karajan was always very meticulous on this audio-visual aspect. Based on his own account, he would sequester himself in the montage room with the technicians for every concert film, meticulously overseeing everything about the film from the light to the sound and from the camera direction to the credits for three whole months.

Von Karajan was intent on ensuring that the millions of people watching the "concert film" at home or in the theater would feel like they, too, were in the concert hall.
To achieve this, both the visual and music quality needed to be perfect. A lack of one of them was out of the question.

Doesn't the same meticulousness also apply to restaurants?
Shouldn't the combination of visuality and taste join together in a journey toward perfection?
In my humble opinion, Per Se is one restaurant that succeeds in doing this.

The restaurant, located in the Time Warner building in Manhattan, has three Michelin stars, but as far as I'm concerned, Per Se is at the top of the list for New York. Why? Because at this place, you'll both enjoy delicious food and have your fill thanks to the visual presentation of the fare. In a market in which quite a few famous chefs play games with customers through their attempts to create ostensible masterpieces and deploy unique cooking techniques (with such endeavors naturally reflected in the price), the success Per Se has attained is not to be underestimated. More to the point, it's a comfortable and elegant restaurant... The tables aren't crammed together; instead, the seats are comfortable, and the view is refreshing, looking out onto Columbus Circle and Central Park.

Like most places, Per Se has the option of a fixed menu. One is standard, while the other is vegetarian. The prices, too, are set; the fact that the prices are set is very important for those that don't like to encounter any nasty surprises afterward. Of course, however, it is extremely expensive. But this is understandable, because the owner and chef is Thomas Keller, an exceptional figure who has won three macaroons with not just Per Se, but also the French Laundry in Napa Valley. As you will appreciate, it's not easy to achieve success, and such things naturally come with a price!

But you could be in for a surprise with the wine. On the wine list that's as thick as a brick, I distinctly remember seeing a wine for the princely sum of 52,000 dollars; if I'm not mistaken, the wine was a Romanée-Conti from 1929. I recall the year, because I had a wine from the same year at home – a white wine produced by the Ankara Agricultural Enterprises, an entity that no longer exists. I left it untouched for years, planning to open the bottle only after grandchildren arrived on the scene. That's what I duly did, but, I must confess, there was nothing particularly remarkable about the taste. Perhaps the wine had gone bad over the years because my son and daughter-in-law lazed about, letting it gather dust above the cupboard at their place. My wine was devoid of impact, but it was inevitable that those opting to sip a 50,000-dollar French wine of the same vintage would leave an impact, at least in their wallets.

If you're out to sample some of the really good stuff from Per Se's comprehensive wine list, you have to be fairly well-positioned at your company because there's no rule that says every bill sent to the company is going to be reimbursed. On the contrary, in the event that you're going to pay for such a wine out of your own pocket, you're either attempting to impress a special someone or hail from either a baking-hot petro-state or the coldest reaches of Siberia. In the event that, like me, you've wondered "what kind of place Per Se is" and accordingly set aside some funds a few months in advance for the pleasure, you'll have to be fairly careful.

But keep an eagle eye out because there are Canadian, Hungarian, Spanish and even French wines for just 80-90 dollars on the massive list – they're tucked in here and there, so you just have to comb carefully to locate them.

But there's no need to talk about the food: Everything offered on the menu is sure to please both the eye and the stomach to the highest degree!

The service is also of similarly high quality. The only mistake with my food was the longish gap between the serving of the fourth and fifth courses. At the same time, they also brought coffee before ice cream, but when they beheld my stare and frown, they immediately rectified the situation without me having to say anything.

After the meal, I found myself humming Beethoven's 7th Symphony as I strolled toward Central Park.
Of course, the maestro directing the orchestra was von Karajan.
His eyes were closed and, as always, he had lost himself in the act of conducting. Sent flying by his movement, his white hair had transformed into snowflakes that were now falling toward the park...

> **"** But you could be in for
> a surprise with the wine. On the
> wine list that's as thick as a brick,
> I distinctly remember seeing
> a wine for the princely sum of
> 52,000 dollars. **"**

# Running Into Sylvie Vartan At Le Stresa

## Le Stresa, Paris

Le Stresa is an Italian restaurant in Paris.

It's located on a street right behind Avenue Montaigne. The region is smack in the middle of famous fashion houses, financial institutions and artistic activities. This area, known as Triangle d'Or (the golden triangle), is one of the wealthier neighborhoods in Paris. That's why the clientele at Le Stresa during the day includes men and women that work in the area and at night, celebrities who live in the neighborhood. That's the reason it has a distinctive clientele. While there are many touristic restaurants a couple of blocks away at Rue Marbeuf and Champs Elysées, Le Stresa is a restaurant that serves its unique clientele – an establishment that rarely sees tourists and keeps them at arm's length when it encounters them.

Le Stresa clearly specifies that Alain Delon and Jean-Paul Belmondo are among the regulars for lunch. The relationship between the restaurant and the actors are so intimate that there is a dish dedicated to each of them on the menu.

We didn't run into them because we went there at night. But we did run into another celebrity.
We had just begun our dinner when seven or eight people, including children, arrived at the table near us. When we looked at the "grandmother" figure receiving the most respect in the group, we recognized her immediately:

It was none other than Sylvie Vartan, the "it girl" of our generation!

The 1960s were the years when teenagers rebelled in America, Britain and France. The rebellion soon spread everywhere, from politics to music.

Youngsters who rebelled and demanded a new and better world were popping up all over the world. Nothing would be better if there weren't young rebels! Nothing that's broken could ever be fixed! The mutiny of the Generation of '68 led to the emergence of great bands, new singers and great songs. These musicians and bands terrorized the world for years.

In North America, legends such as Joan Baez, Bob Dylan, Jimmy Hendrix, Simon and Garfunkel and Leonard Cohen began singing about things people had never heard of.

In Britain, bands such as The Beatles, The Rolling Stones, The Animals and The Moody Blues soon followed.

This trend manifested itself in France with names like Johnny Hallyday, Sylvie Vartan and Françoise Hardy. They were followed by Jane Birkin-Serge Gainsbourg, Michel Polnareff, Jacques Dutronc, Hugues Aufray, Sheila, Claude François, Richard Anthony and George Moustaki.
Celebrities such as Charles Aznavour, Gilbert Bécaud, Georges Brassens, Mireille Mathieu, Serge Reggiani, Yves Montand, Jacques Brel and Dalida now appealed to the middle aged, while Édith Piaf ended up with tourists at Bateaux Mouches.

Youngsters had rebelled for a better future. They wanted the old to be replaced with the new!
And Sylvie Vartan was one of the stars that shone during this period.
When this blonde, petite girl with separated teeth sang "Ce soir je serai la plus belle pour aller danser" (Tonight I'll be the most beautiful girl at the dance), it felt like she was taking us with her at a time when we couldn't even find a girl whose hand to hold, let alone take to a dance. Dreaming aside, in reality, we typically even went to our high school prom just as guys!
Just then:
We were back at our prom, and here was that blonde, petite girl with separated teeth! As we looked around in bewilderment, certain it must be a dream, we suddenly understood it was not when we encountered the harsh look of her husband, Johnny Hallyday!
They were in Istanbul for a concert and were staying at the hotel where our prom was being held. Our very resourceful concert organizers had somehow managed to persuade the famous couple to come to our hall. (These friends were resourceful indeed. They had managed to get many celebrities like Adamo, Ajda Pekkan, Alpay, Marino Marini and Peppino di Capri to give concerts at our 250-person-capacity Tevfik Fikret Hall!)
The couple left the ball after chatting with us for a while.
As the most beautiful girl at the ball, Sylvie had proven her point in her song!

At Le Stresa, they had a quiet dinner as a family. In fact, I believe it was the birthday of one of the kids. They celebrated without disturbing anyone.
Before leaving, I thought about saying a few words since we were "old pals" but I refrained from talking. Sometimes grandmothers don't want anyone to mention their age!

# Memories Of Cannes
# Escapades At Le Divellec

## Le Divellec, Paris

Le Divellec, famous for its seafood, is within walking distance of the French National Assembly in Paris. Politicians, statesmen, diplomats and senior civil servants are all regulars.
We went there before it was sold to the Costes Group, when Monsieur Le Divellec was still running the place.

My wife and I ordered an aperitif while awaiting our son's arrival. He was in Cannes to see the film festival and was coming by train to meet us. We knew the train had arrived and were counting the minutes until the arrival of his taxi.
While waiting for him, I remembered one of my own trips to Cannes.

I was a student then, sharing a flat in Paris with two other friends. One night we polished off a large bottle of rakı – which was never a liquor that was easy to find.
This remarkable event had made us dizzy with ideas, prompting us to search for something to do to celebrate this victory.
What could we do?
A nightclub? So dull!
Visit friends in Lausanne? We were there just last week!
Then someone suggested: There's a film festival in Cannes. How about going there, where some fairly attractive girls were sure to be waiting for us?
We all loved the idea. If you have a good idea, you'll certainly find others to embrace it...
We duly looked at a map, which confronted us with the reality that the Côte d'Azur was 1,000 kilometers

away.

But we had just finished a whole bottle of rakı!

I asked my friends:

"Can any of you drive for two hours?"

As soon as the affirmative response came, we rushed out and stopped at the café on the corner. I gulped down a glass of rum and threw myself into the back seat and dozed off.

I was roused from my slumber precisely two hours later. My friend who was driving refused to even give me five extra minutes. I took the wheel and put my foot on the gas.

The next morning upon our arrival, I parked the car in a parking lot in Croisette and woke my friends up. A Deux Cheveaux, the trademark car of students at that time, was rocking back and forth next to us. I looked and saw a couple making love. I pretended not to see them and said to my friends:

"Rock the car guys, this is Cannes. Let's not be strangers."

Just then, our son made his entrance to Le Divellec, waking me up from my reverie. We embraced. That rash action from my youth could have had grave and even tragic consequences. I could have ended up with no son and no lunch at Le Divellec!

I hugged my son again. It was time to order. I asked for salted sea bass, while my wife and son ordered turbot.

The turbot was unique. No wonder Monsieur Le Divellec was so famous. Unfortunately, the turbot went cold as the waiter was ceremoniously breaking the salt off my fish.

But so what? The one who went from Paris to Cannes and the one who came from Cannes to Paris are alive and well. Who cares if the fish is cold!

# Running The Rule On My Favorite Restaurants

## New York, London, Paris, San Francisco

I got talking once with a student of mine who was doing her graduate studies.

She was 41... She'd risen to the post of general manager of a well-known financial organization, but she'd never married.

"Why?" I asked one day.

"Sir, don't take this the wrong way, but I don't trust men anymore."

Of course I didn't take offense, as I've always seen myself as a trustable man.

She had had several relationships and had always encountered similar behavior: loutishness, egotism and a catalogue of impertinence stemming from a desire to impose oneself. And, of course, cheating...

"It all really wore me down," she continued. "I just want to be myself and have some peace!"

"You just haven't found the right person; otherwise, marriage isn't such a bad thing!" I responded.

"Sir, I'm not against marriage. Do you think I found someone like you but decided not to tie the knot?" (I can't entirely remember if she actually said this complimentary sentence or whether it remained in my memory like this. Years have passed since this conservation, so I might have forgotten.)

The crux of the matter is that we men are a difficult lot! (But don't rush off and jump to the conclusion that women are angels who are "easy to get along with" based on such a categorization.) We are a breed that's in the wrong when we're young; we have many deficiencies and make many mistakes. What's worse is that we show no inclination to resolve the matter! Our "difficult" nature stems from this tendency to avoid change and refuse to accept our faults or rectify our mistakes.

You can't but help give my student her due. But the other side of the coin is that young guys just aren't capable of knowing any of this. Trying to explain this to her, I said:

"I understand your independent and free lifestyle, but if you ask me, don't avoid finding a man! There should be someone in your life at your side. People need someone of the opposite sex (or maybe of the same sex) in their life for when they fall down, someone to talk to when they're in a bind and someone to console them when they're upset. More to the point, you really feel the need for this when you get older. Loneliness entails weakness! When you're on your own at home at night and someone knocks on the door, you worry about who it is. If there's a man at home, you can say, "The door's ringing... Go get it." This comfort and security alone outweighs the difficulties of a life together. Think about it."

The thing I tried to relate to my student doesn't just go for relationships between men and women but highlights something that we need to feel all the time in our daily lives: Safety and security and the peace that comes with this.

Wining and dining is no different! Don't you want to go to a restaurant where you'll trust the quality and the personnel's behavior? At least I do. Will the meze be off, are they going to take me for a ride on the bill, will the waiters irritate me? I wonder about all of this. Wouldn't you want to eat at a place with peace and enjoyment instead of entertaining such worries? That's why I don't usually opt for newly opened restaurants. Such places are like young guys who are completely unpredictable. It's never clear when they'll do what! Let me wait so that they can settle down and figure out who they are... Then let me be sure that they'll make me happy so that we can be together! Chatterboxes who go, "Hey, there's this new place that's really trendy – everyone's there and the food is amazing!" have nothing to say to me!

I want what I know!

With this in mind, here are the restaurants that I love, trust and enjoy going to in the cities that I visit the most:

New York: Eleven Mad, Blue Hill Stone Borns

San Francisco: Chez Panisse

Paris: Apicius, Le Clarence

London: Dinner by Heston Blumenthal

These are all expensive restaurants. It's not easy to go there – you need to save up the money!

But please answer with all honesty: What love is easy to attain? What love doesn't require one heck of a lot of work?

# The Bride From Rome

## Al Moro, Rome

It's tiring to walk in Rome.

After being on our feet all day, we sat down at the highly recommended Al Moro and ordered our proseccos and food.

Fontana Di Trevi... Piazza Navona... The Pantheon... The Colosseum... San Pietro... no... no... no... We didn't get to these sights that tourists fill but never vacate.

Instead, we toured around Parioli, the neighborhood of the rich and famous in Rome. We now know which buildings were constructed by the people of the Roman Empire and how they lived. We were curious about how people lived in these buildings now and what they ate and drank, so we perused all the streets to see how the eternal city was inhabited, not exhibited. We tried to understand how the Romans lived their daily lives. We toured "the living Rome" until we were ready to drop dead.

Among the cheerful Italians dining in the charming garden of Trattoria Al Moro, our main course arrived between proseccos and red wine. It was a meat dish whose Italian name I forgot... Accompanying the meat was mashed potatoes, which some restaurants sometimes provide on the house.
I cut a piece of meat and devoured it: Wow... Delicious...

I sampled some of the mashed potatoes... I stopped... Took another bite... Stopped again... Then I said to my wife, "These are Carla's mashed potatoes."

She looked at me as if to say, "What are you talking about?" I explained:

It was the start of the 1950s... We were among the crowds that were waiting for the boat at Galata Pier's International Lines. My grandfather, grandmother, aunt, my mother and little me! The passengers of the boat also included my uncle and his fiancée. The prospective bride was coming to Turkey from Italy...

During that time, all Istanbul had to offer were mosques such as as Hahgia Sophia, Sultanahmet and Süleymaniye, the Grand Bazaar, palaces like Topkapı, Dolmabahçe and Beylerbeyi and scenic beauty in the form of the Bosporus. If I tell you that the first big hotel in the city, the Hilton, was opened in 1958, I believe it will be easier to picture the city at that time.

People were conservative and mostly closed to the outside world. The number of people who knew a foreign language was probably less than the number in Tokyo. Our family was also Muslim, but it consisted of members who made an attempt to be less conservative and adhere to a Western way of life that they knew little about. My grandmother used to cover her head when she went out. My aunt and my mother didn't. They used to brag about being the modern girls of the Turkish Republic.

Our future bride was coming to Turkey after accepting a very different world and a whole different environment.

Why?

Because my uncle was exceedingly handsome...

He had graduated from the academy as an architect and went to Rome for post-graduate studies. Carla, the bride-to-be, was the daughter of the owner of the guesthouse he was staying at. They had met, fallen in love and decided to get married.

My grandparents didn't approve of their handsome and cultured son getting married to a girl who had a different religion, culture and language. During that time, we didn't have concepts like the "clash of civilizations," or they weren't of the type that would rip societies apart. Still, mothers want to choose their future daughters-in-law themselves and wanted the candidate to be amiable (and easily controllable, whether directly or indirectly) and have the ability to look after their sons. Of course, beauty came into play, too. The tradition of a possible daughter-in-law being taken to a Turkish bath and being seen naked by the groom's female family members is an ancient custom in Anatolia that was concocted to counteract deception.

Yes, my grandparents did not approve of this marriage, but they never openly protested...

That's why we were all stressed when the boat from Italy docked at Galata Pier. Since we didn't have Skype, FaceTime or similar communication tools, we had only seen Carla from pictures that arrived via air mail a week after being sent. She was a young, vibrant, cute girl. But what about her character? This was something we could only find out here!

We were nervous! Or rather, the elderly were stressed... There is no room for this kind of concern in the pure world of children!

My mother and aunt constantly advised my grandparents not to give the girl a cold shoulder.

The ship had docked and the passengers had started to disembark. Just then "our bunch" appeared from the parted door of the customs section.

My grandfather straightened his tie... My grandmother loosened her headscarf a little and pushed it back to reveal the top of her hair... My mother and aunt ensured their attire was orderly... I, on the other hand, repeated the two Italian words I had learned to impress our "guest."

My uncle and Carla started walking toward us. My grandfather picked up his bouquet of flowers, which had started to show signs of wilting because we had been standing there for two hours, from the bench... We were ready!

All of a sudden, Carla let go of my uncle's hand, started running toward us and hugged my grandmother tightly:
"Mamma mia!"

We all learned that "mamma" meant "mother" in Italian.
My grandmother came undone at that exact moment and said with tears in her eyes "My daughter... My child..." Carla had been promoted from candidate to bride!

My grandfather, with bouquet in hand, was waiting for the love-fest between bride and mother-in-law to end. I don't know where he got the idea from, but he first kissed Carla's hand and, as if to say, "We know these things as well as the Italians," he said, "My dear daughter, welcome to your new home."
When it was their turn, my mother and aunt said, "Welcome sister," and embraced the new bride...
I, on the other hand, was baffled by the excitement and the unexpected turn of events. Instead of my previously prepared line of "Ben arrivato signorina," I could only shout, "Welcome, Auntie."

The congenial Roman bride quickly got used to Istanbul and her new family... We all adored her... We learned so much from her... But what impressed me the most was the taste of her mashed potatoes which she made calmly when my uncle's friends showed up unannounced. She made the same tasty mashed potatoes until the day she died!

Angela mia!

> 66 My uncle and Carla started walking toward us. My grandfather picked up his bouquet of flowers, which had started to show signs of wilting because we had been standing there for two hours, from the bench... We are ready! All of sudden, Carla let go of my uncle's hand, started running toward us and hugged my grandmother tighly: "Mamma mia!" 99

# From Le Relais
# To Ismet Baba

## Le Relais, Lugano

I was tired.
I wanted nothing more than to go rest somewhere quiet and tranquil.
We duly headed to Lugano and set up camp at the Villa Castagnola.

The trip, which included a stopover in Milan, had been somewhat tiring. After freshening up and taking in the view of the lake from our window, we descended to Le Relais for a wonderful dinner. We didn't leave a tip, mind you, as I had reckoned that giving a big, full tip on the last day would be a better idea given that the restaurant didn't seem to have many customers anyway. In seeing the frown on the waiter's face, however, I realized my course of action might not have been the correct one.

Still, when I opened the balcony window the following morning, allowing the scent of the nearby flowers to merge with the fantastic view of the lake and its surrounding mountains, I could scarcely contain myself.
"I think we've landed in heaven," I pronounced to my wife.

How wrong I would be!

Following breakfast, we grabbed a couple of lounge chairs on the grass next to the lake and opened our books.
"You're right, I think we've landed in heaven," my wife said, agreeing with my assertion.

How wrong she would be!
Not long after, the phone rang: It was the manager of our apartment building.

"Someone's unfortunately broken into your place," he said. "But it appears there's no mess. Nothing is missing."

My wife hung up, and we considered the situation. If there wasn't much missing, there was little sense in leaving this paradise and returning home. After all, we'd seen a lot in our day...

We called my office, and an assistant headed to our place immediately to radio in a report: "They came in through the door... Everything's normal in the sitting room. The office looks normal, and they didn't touch the books... And there's nothing out of the ordinary in the other rooms or the bathroom."

"The bedroom, go look at the bedroom!" we cried.

"I'm looking now," the assistant said.

"What do you see?"

"Everything's normal!"

"For crying out loud, what kind of break-in is this? Is the safe still there?" we asked.

"What safe?"

"Isn't there a safe between the bed and the dresser?" we inquired with growing trepidation.

"No, unfortunately," came the reply.

We learned what had happened from the papers a few days later: a gang consisting of one woman and two men sporting elegant clothing and a high-end vehicle had been breaking into houses in our area. They hadn't taken anything from anywhere except the safes.

This time my wife started to cry: all her jewelry was in that safe.

None of the jewelry was particularly expensive, but we had struggled in our life, acquiring everything with difficulty. We had saved up our pennies earned with sweat and tears, buying these modest pieces of jewelry, whose sentimental value far exceeded any monetary one.

We felt awful as heaven turned into hell.

With no reason to stay, we elected to return home. We found seats on a plane departing the day after. With no other choice, we again went to the soulless Relais – the most elegant place of the three places to eat in Villa Castagnola.

Le Relais is a classic, fancy-schmancy restaurant harkening back to La Belle Époque. It asks customers to come to dine in attire that befits the restaurant's style. It also has good food and a broad wine menu.

In our state, however, what we really needed was a different type of restaurant to "beat the blues" – something like a Greek taverna or a Turkish meyhane by the seaside where you can sit yourself down and let the sound of the waves wash over you. And after a couple of glasses of ouzo or rakı, you'll loosen up, forget your worries and leave without a care in the world.

Le Relais is certainly not a restaurant in which you can "beat the blues." You can't have some risotto and wine and cast all your worries away. Instead, we ate out of need. As we left, I left a tip for two days, eliciting a sparkle in place of a frown on the face of the waiter. All of it showed that he was capable of seeing off a customer with a smile.

But a good meyhane in which to beat the blues is İsmet Baba on the Bosphorus, the slice of paradise that separates Europe and Asia. Sitting across from you is an age-old history that starts with Topkapı Palace, continues with the Haghia Sophia and Blue Mosque and goes all the way to the palaces of Dolmabahçe and Çırağan. In front of your lies a sea that never rests, and on your plate lies fish that was freshly caught that day. Next to that is your white cheese and rakı. Perhaps these aren't enough to transport you to paradise, but there's no question that they'll extricate you from whatever hell you find yourself in at the moment.

On your way in or out, you can see the small portrait photos of a few people. All of them are the photos of the meyhane's "evening guys" who have taken their leave of this world. Blind Seyfı, Father Kadri, Carpenter Vasil, Captain Abbas, Fisherman Pandelli, Painter Peres and Hot-Headed Mehmet are just a few of those whose photos are here. The photographs are indeed one of the most characteristic things about İsmet Baba.

Sometimes, I've wondered if my likeness will one day grace the little vitrine as well, but probably not: To get pride of place for one's picture, you have to have been one of the regulars honored with the distinction of being an "evening guy." And these guys were serious, having imbibed their rakı at İsmet Baba almost every evening, come what may. When I was at school, I never got on the honor roll, and I don't reckon I'll get a similar honor given that I just can't keep up appearances with the likes of the Blind Seyfis of the world.

But even if there's only a small chance in winning the distinction, it doesn't hurt to try. So, if you'll excuse me, I have to find a table before the sun goes down…

> "What do you see?"
> "Everything's normal!"
> "For crying out loud, what kind of break-in is this? Is the safe still there?" we asked.
> "What safe?"

Photo by Niyazi Gurgen

# My Restaurant Evaluation Manifesto And Le Clarence

## Le Clarence, Paris

I'm not that curious about food or drink. I only eat a little, and I generally prefer my wife's meals.
I go to restaurants a lot but not to find good and unique food. That's certainly important, but my main reason in going out to eat is to join and converse with others at unique establishments.

Around these parts, the Mediterranean sun really gets the blood moving and the mouths talking – to the point that if you're sitting together with people you enjoy talking to, digging into some freshly caught fish and downing a drink or two, you won't just wonder how the time flies but how life itself is flying by! People have so much to say to each other, but they also need to understand each other. For this, you need a suitable atmosphere. If you find yourself in an enjoyable ambiance while eating your dinner, you'll never grow tired of the conversation.

The true taste of a meal comes from the conversation itself! As far as I'm concerned, a good restaurant is one that fosters a good conversation.
The quality of the salt, sugar or drink in a meal varies according to everyone's tastes. I like eating stuffed peppers with garlic yoghurt, but it would hardly be fair to call out a restaurant for serving me the dish without any yoghurt. With that in mind, I steer clear of any such evaluations that begrudge the respect for all the effort that's gone into the meal. Moreover, if you've passed judgement on a restaurant after eating there just once, how valid do you think your evaluation will be for any generalization? At a restaurant, even the same menu and the same recipes can come out differently depending on who's making the meal. What the head chef cooks up is one thing, and what the deputy cooks up is another! The same goes for a chef who opens different restaurants: the standard of quality can never be the same.

For me, the main criterion is whether or not the restaurant provides what I'm really after: an enjoyable atmosphere for conversation.

I start sizing a place up to determine whether it fulfills this condition when I make the reservation. After that comes the process of evaluating the establishment. Things like the location, how I'm greeted, how I'm shown to my seat, the table and seating arrangement, the decoration, the overall comfort, the quality of the clientele, the attitude of the servers, the state of the washrooms, the suitability of the music (where applicable), the price-quality comparison and, finally, how they bid me farewell are all important to me. If all of these suit me, if they've given me a chance to enjoy a nice conversation and, naturally, if the food and drink are in accordance with my tastes (i.e., I'm not saying "if the food and drink are good"), then that place is a "good restaurant" for me!

This might be a fine dining restaurant or, on the opposite end of the scale, it might be an intimate Japanese izakaya. It might be a simple Spanish tapas bar, a Parisian bistro with joined tables, a Greek taverna with music or a run-down Turkish meyhane next to the water. It's enough that the place – regardless of whatever class of restaurant it belongs to – is "good" according to the aforementioned checklist.

Le Clarence is an establishment in the fine - dining class that gets top marks from me – just like Apicius elsewhere in Paris, New York's Eleven Mad or Blue Hill at Stone Barns, San Francisco's Chez Panisse or London's Dinner by Heston Blumenthal.

Built in 1884, Le Clarence is a hotel restaurant located in a small mansion in an upmarket Parisian quarter. The mansion itself belongs to Prince Robert de Luxembourg, the owner of Château Haut-Brion. With its carpets that lend a sense of gentility, the wood paneling, the wall ornaments, the crystal chandeliers and valuable artwork, it's an apt representative of French luxury, pomp and elegance.

And as far as I'm concerned, it's essential to lose yourself in the big couches next to the chimney on the second floor and have an aperitif. After this magnificent and relaxing start, it's time to eat food with real silverware in one of the halls – all three of which sit only 35 people combined. We, in the end, ate in the Pontac library room.

The restaurant was opened at the end of 2015 by chef Christophe Pelé, who scored two Michelin stars at a previous restaurant of his. Unsurprisingly, Le Clarence quickly attained the same level of success – but I wouldn't be surprised if it earns itself another star in the near future.

Ultimately, the fantastic flavors of food from the land and the sea, the rich wine cellar (it's heavy on Domaine Clarence Dillon but offers other domestic and international wines as well), the grace of the language used in reservation confirmations, the polite and expert service and – despite all of this – the unexaggerated price (and even the elegance of the physical bill itself) all make Le Clarence the "perfect" restaurant as far my criteria are concerned.

# The Carpenter And The American

## Orfoz, Bodrum

Everyone's view on life is different, and there's one anecdote about this that I particularly like:

A young and intelligent American comes to Bodrum (probably from Silicon Valley – back in the day, I would have said he was from New York, but the bright and ambitious American youth of today all seem to be from San Francisco). Following a bout of swimming on a warm summer evening, he went searching for a restaurant for some dinner; on his way, he spied a carpenter's shop featuring a unique and gorgeous chair in front of the door. Just beside that was a man in a cap sitting in a wicker chair, twirling rosary beads and watching the passersby.

Seeking to ingratiate himself, the American offered a "Merhaba" in Turkish before speaking to the presumed carpenter. "Is this chair for sale?" he asked.
"No, it's not. That was a special order," he replied.
"Are you a carpenter?" our American asked.
"Yep."
"Is this your shop?"
"Yep."
"Do you always make chairs like this?"
"I do."
"How quickly can you can make a chair like this?"
"In a week."
"How much do they go for?"

The carpenter gave his reply. After the bright young thing from Silicon Valley considered the length of time and did the exchange rate, he turned back to the master carpenter.

"How many people work for you?"

"I have an apprentice, and that's it."

"So what would happen if you had 10 apprentices?"

"Whatever would I do that for?"

"For this: If you had 10 apprentices, you could increase your capacity, produce more and earn more," the Silicon Valley man said.

"What am I going to do when I earn more money?"

"What do you mean, 'What am I going to do?' You'll enjoy yourself and take it easy!"

"What did I do to deserve this smart aleck?" he seemed to say as he twirled his beads once more before giving his real answer:

"Look, mate, what on earth do you think I'm doing right now?" the carpenter said.

The young American probably failed to find anything "acceptable" in this philosophy of a slow-paced life. For his part, the carpenter probably couldn't understand the "logic" in exerting blood, sweat and tears just so he could acquire what he already had.

I do wonder, did the American find a world suited to his tastes when he finally made it to the restaurant? If he went to Orfoz in Bodrum, he probably did. The place is run by – no lie – a family of chemists. They had worked in a different city in the past before opening a small shop in Bodrum, where they grew their business; later, they opened a place that leans toward seafood. In time, they increased their customer capacity. The prices are high, but I think it's a restaurant that pleases both the diner and the provider. In a jargon comprehensible to the American, it's a win-win.

They offer a fixed tasting menu, but diners can also make small changes if they so desire. And if they do make changes, it won't change the price much, since Orfoz offers fresh food depending on the season – so there's not really a menu with a wide variety of options. What they do have frequently is mussels with parmesan, sea snails and blue crab. The last time I went, Çağlar, one of the owners, offered me some of his home-made white wine, although I'm of the opinion that it would be better as an apéro than a drink alongside the meal.

Are there no problems with Orfoz? Of course there are: You're issued with only one fork and knife from start to finish, there are no separate plates for salad even though the plates are small, the service can sometimes be hasty and orders are occasionally mixed up. In my opinion, the basic problem is that the place doesn't know if it's a fine-dining restaurant or a meyhane – that's something the owners must decide. After all, there are elements of both at Orfoz. If they were to decide and move in one direction or the other accordingly, it would be possible to clear up all the problems.

Orfoz is a "good" restaurant. With a bit of effort, it could be promoted to the league of "really good" restaurants.

# Do Silk Shirts Eat Soup?

## Peter Lugar, New York

Nasreddin Hodja is a trickster known in many places around the world. As it was, he was a folk philosopher from Anatolia whose funny anecdotes got one laughing – and thinking.

One evening, while the hodja was going home, he happened upon a house from which the sounds of music and uproarious laughter were coming. He brought his donkey (which he invariably rode backwards) to a stop and listened closely. Someone at the door invited him in to the festivities inside – a wedding, in this case. The hodja tied his donkey to a tree and entered the house. They had set up tables in the crowded interior garden, where everyone was eating, drinking and making merry. No one paid him any attention; he waited a bit, but when no one beckoned him to a table, he grew tired of the proceedings, took his leave and headed home.

When he arrived home, he removed his normal attire and put on his most ostentatious garb. Sporting a radiant silk shirt, he returned to the wedding. This time, the guests who saw him in such finery crowded around him, bid him welcome and sat him down at the head table. Everyone else at the table all saluted him with respect. The servants, too, immediately brought the hodja some of the choicest morsels of food. With food on his plate, Nasreddin Hodja turned to those assembled, wished them a pleasant meal and proceeded to dunk the sleeve of his silk shirt in the soup.

"Hodja!" they exclaimed. "What on earth are you doing? Your shirt's fallen into the soup!"

In a quiet voice, he answered: "My shirt hasn't fallen into the soup, my shirt's having some soup!"

"My goodness! Hodja, would a shirt ever eat soup?" they responded.

"It would, it would," the hodja said.

"Just a moment ago, I came in my normal clothes, and no one looked me in the face. Now, when all of you saw my silk shirt and golden necklace, everyone started to take an interest in me. It seems that the thing that's worthy isn't me but my shirt. It follows, then, that it deserves to have the soup and eat the food, no?"

Some restaurants pay a lot of attention to their customers' attire. Places with lots of stars on their shoulder sometimes take the matter to the extreme. When I'm at a good restaurant, I don't like seeing fellow diners in blue jeans and T-shirts. But that doesn't mean that it's only a jacket and a tie that lends chic and elegance. In the past, those that had the right to enter army-run restaurants were required to do so in a tie. But those that came without ties were furnished with one at the coat check, allowing them to "fulfill" the rule. But that meant that the general scene was this: A bunch of men in T-shirts who had donned ties that had been worn by hundreds of others and probably been stained just as many times by the food!
It might have a Michelin star on its shoulder, but Brooklyn's Peter Luger Steakhouse is one restaurant that is relaxed on this front with its customers. Diners get to enjoy their food in comfortable attire, while the wait staff offer pleasant service without getting tense, fixing their customers with an icy stare or angering the clientele.

The only problem is the burnt meat. Most of the customers that come there – like most in America – want meat that is seared on the outside. It's true, the insides of the meat are like cotton, but the exterior is like coal. In the end, I've never been able to understand why people insist on continuing to eat food like this and fill restaurants like this to the gills, even though American doctors, as well as the media who have shared their warnings, have implored people to not eat burnt meat on account of the huge cancer risk.
What can I say: My God grant everyone good health!

> " Just a moment ago, I came in my normal clothes, and no one looked me I the face. Now, when all of you saw my silk shirt and golden necklace, everyone started to take an interest in me. It seems that the thing that's worthy isn't me but my shirt. It follows, then, that it deserves to have the soup and eat the food, no?"

# Is This Place Going To Flood?

## Wolseley, London

When we first went to London, we used to stay at the Hyde Park Hotel, only for it to later close. It would subsequently reopen as the Mandarin Oriental, but we never went. Instead, we started heading to the Ritz, but I was not much for the place, which was as old as the elderly women downstairs sipping their five cups of tea and nibbling on their cakes at tea time. The concierge, meanwhile, had appeared in the film Notting Hill, providing him with all the pretentiousness that you would expect.

While staying at the Ritz, I discovered Wolseley, a charming café-restaurant that was close to the hotel. One day, I was at Wolseley with a friend when the sky turned dark, quickly producing a downpour.
"Do you know that this place was a car dealership when it first opened?" my friend said as we chatted.
"You're kidding me. This elegant place used to be a car dealership?" I said as the cloudburst outside increased in intensity.
I didn't notice myself, but a smile had appeared on my lips. "Why are you laughing?" my friend asked.
"Do you think this place might flood?"
"What kind of question is that?" he exclaimed. "Why would it flood? What would make you think of that?"

I explained:
My older brother, a law professor at Paris' Nanterre University, had taken advantage of the Easter break to come and visit. At the time, we were living in an apartment by the sea; like many seaside towns on the Mediterranean, there was just a narrow street between our place and the water. It was a night of food, drink and great conversation over the fare we had prepared – all the food my brother had missed while in France. Suddenly, the sky darkened and the heavens opened. Over the course of our meal, the rain only grew in

144

strength instead of tapering off. It was a jaw-dropping sight, the likes of which we'd never seen before. After finishing our meal, we made our way to the front and settled into the chairs by the window with new drinks. The sea had swallowed the street to the extent that you could no longer tell what was water and what was road. It was raining cats and dogs, the sky was roaring, lightning was flashing and thunder was rumbling. We were more than content to behold the sight in a warm house with drink in hand, even as we murmured a prayer that God would spare the less fortunate who might be caught in the tempest.

The morning after, however, we realized – to our wide-eyed amazement – that we were not among those that God had spared. The apartment's custodian came to bring us the bad news: The garage beneath the apartment had flooded, and all the vehicles had been inundated!

Because none of us had ever experienced anything like it, it hadn't occurred to any of us that our cars might be flooded by such a storm. It was clear, however, that our cars had been drowning as we were enjoying ourselves upstairs!

"You've got insurance, right?" my brother asked.

"Thank God, yes."

"Then there's no reason to worry."

The reason to worry would only rear its ugly head later: The insurance didn't cover flooding!

My car at the time was an expensive vehicle that had the newest electronic controls. I maintained hope against hope that nothing had happened to it or that we would escape with only a bit of damage.

And what did they say when I finally got the car towed to a mechanic?

"I'm sorry to say, but the car's totaled."

"What do you mean 'totaled?' It's an expensive car with electronic controls!"

"That's why it's totaled!" came the response. "If it had been a cheap, normal car, we could have worked it out, but stuff like this with electronic controls unfortunately goes kaput!"

For crying out loud, I thought to myself: If only I had bought a car with an ox for a motor instead of one of those expensive ones with smart electronic controls!

But then again, there was always the chance that something like that would get mad cow disease...

But getting angry or even going crazy wasn't going to fix anything.

"So what you're saying is that this car has zero value now, is that right?" I inquired.

"Yes, so long as you don't count the towing and labor costs. If you add those too, you're into the negative!"

Meanwhile, back in London, the rain was continuing – when I had learned that the place used to house cars, the trip to the mechanic had inevitably come to mind.

"There's no reason to worry; this place won't flood," my friend assured me.

At least this time we escaped with only a bit of damage to the wallet...

# The 8-Year-Old Fugitive

## Beyti, Istanbul

Beyti was one of Istanbul's first steakhouses, and I reckon it remains – deservedly so – the most famous of such establishments.

I've been going to there since the 1960s. In those days, it was just a simple, tiny meat restaurant located far from the center of Istanbul. In time, however, it moved closer to the main airport, Atatürk International, becoming a destination with three floors, lots of tables and elegant decoration. Still, it never lost any of its old character; even though it has the potential to host several hundred people at the same time, it's shown that it's capable of welcoming customers without any drop-off in food or service.

The architect of this success is undoubtedly Beyti Güler, who has been at the helm since 1945. Mr. Güler is known for his expertise in raising the animals, his cooking, as well as his politeness and honesty. Because of these qualities, the reputation of Beyti has never been questioned, even when a number of different steakhouses were opened in the city in subsequent years – some of which even opened branches overseas. Beyti has continued to be a must-stop for presidents, artists and everyone during a visit to Istanbul. In both Europe and America, there are few places whose meat I like more.

One time, I went there alone – for reasons that I can no longer remember. In the mood for lamb chops, I told the waiter: "I just want a green salad on the side; don't give me anything else."
My four lamb chops and salad came, and I was about to dig in when I suddenly stopped.
I beckoned the waiter over once more. "Do you have a banana?" I asked.
"Of course we do, sir," he said, though he was caught a bit off guard by a question about bananas just as I

was about to get eating.

"Would you like it now?" he continued.

"Yes, right away!" I exclaimed.

Even if the waiter couldn't make heads or tails of my request, he respectfully fulfilled my desire. With the banana procured, I began my meal.

My parents split when I was very young – in fact, I don't even remember the event. My father was an officer while my mother found a job at the Istanbul Chamber of Commerce after the divorce. I stayed with her – along with my grandma and grandpa, aunts and uncles – at my grandfather's big wooden house by the Bosphorus. All of them helped take care of me when my mother went to work during the day.

Come the weekend, I would go see my father, who was teaching some sort of class on war strategy at the military academy. While my mother was a bit of an authoritarian, my father, somewhat unexpectedly, was a tolerant, happy-go-lucky officer. During my weekends with him, he would never let me do my homework; instead, he'd take me to the football ground, theater or circus. On Saturday nights, we'd go for a father-son dinner at some modest fish restaurant along the Bosphorus. He also told me that he always trusted me and that, come what may, I would do well in my classes regardless.

I had spent yet another weekend in such a fashion when I got back to my mother's on Sunday evening.

"Did you do your homework?" she asked before she'd even given me a hug.

"I did," I said fearfully, even though, as you might expect, I had not.

She asked me to show her. "Just a second, let me go the washroom," I said, stalling for time.

I went to the washroom; after coming to the conclusion that there was no one in the vicinity, I surreptitiously exited – leaving the light on to suggest that I was still inside – before escaping the house!

I was 8 years old.

I made my way to the pier; while waiting for the ferry, I saw an uncle and his family in the area.

"What are you doing on the street at this hour?" they asked.

"I've come to get some bread," I answered before quickly making myself scarce.

When the ferry came, I jumped on and headed for Üsküdar. From there I boarded another ferry and crossed from Asia over to Europe. I then got on a bus in Beşiktaş and soon arrived at the military academy.

I immediately surrendered myself to the sentry at the gate. "I am the son of General Staff Col. Cahit Tanör," I said.

By that time, it was 9 at night and everyone back home had been thrown into a state of panic when they couldn't find me.

My father embraced me affectionately and called my mother to say that I had arrived safety and that she shouldn't worry.

I stayed with my father for six months. Because he was unmarried, he lived at the academy's lodgings, which used to be part of Sultan Abdülhamid's Yıldız Palace. They assigned me a bed and registered me at a primary school nearby; in so doing, I spent six months as an 8-year-old completing mandatory visiting service at the military academy.

We would eat our lunch at the academy's canteen, while dinner was in my father's lodgings. He would eat simple things and down a couple of glasses or rakı. For me, though, they prepared a menu that was in accordance with the conditions of the facility: Lamb chops, green salad and bananas. For six months, this is the only thing I ate for dinner (to this day, these are my favorite things alongside rakı). The other things I would have were meatballs and fried eggplant when we went to the modest little fish restaurant on Saturday evenings.

My mother and father were never in the same place – they never showed me affection at the same time. But what can one do? That's sometimes what life throws at you. Like a lot of emotions, affection isn't distributed to everyone equally.

Back at the Beyti, I grabbed the waiter's attention again. With eyes seemingly wondering what this strangest of customers was going to ask for now, he approached.
"Could I have a glass of rakı?" I inquired.

The lamb chops, green salad and banana were for me. The rakı was for my father...

> 66 "Did you do your homework?"
> my mother asked before she'd given me
> a hug. "I did," I said fearfully, even
> though, as you might expect, I had not.
> She asked me to Show her. "Just a
> second, let me go to the washroom",
> I said, stalling for time. 99

# RESTAURANTS *and* TALES

Made in the
USA
Columbia, SC